Love Treatments for the Body of Christ

Pastor Chrissy Carter

LOVE TREATMENTS FOR THE BODY OF CHRIST.

Please direct all copyright inquiries to:
B.O.Y. Enterprises, Inc.
c/o Author Copyrights
P.O. Box 1012
Lowell, NC 28098

Paperback ISBN: 978-1-955605-17-5

Cover and Interior Design: B.O.Y. Enterprises, Inc.

Printed in the United States.

Acknowledgements

To my Heavenly Father, thank you for loving me enough to send Your only begotten Son to die in my place so that I may experience a new life in Christ Jesus.

To my Savior and Lover of my very soul, Jesus Christ, thank You for modeling and showcasing love for me to imitate. I will forever strive to love like You!

To my Comforter and Guide, the Amazing Holy Spirit that you are, I can do nothing apart from You. I'm grateful for Your patience and Your Truth, and if You didn't reveal the how to me, the direction for this book, it would only be a thought.

To my amazing husband and friend, Henry Carter, I love you and I'm grateful you believed in Christ's presence in me to step out and lay hold to this assignment.

To all my children, grandchildren, mother, uncles, aunties, siblings, nephews and nieces, cousins, friends, AND TO UNITY AND LOVE MINISTRIES AKA "THE LOVE HOUSE," I love every one of you!

Special thanks to my publisher B.O.Y Enterprises, Nilvia Felipe, and TJ Austin.

Table of Contents

Foreword

Prophetess and Pastor Chrissy Carter has been my sister in Christ and friend for over 17 years. Oh, how I can see now how divine intervention brought us together. Under the guise of a hairstylist, GOD slipped her right into my journey of life in Him. At the time, I was so hungry to learn more about God, to understand with greater depth His Word, and to have a deep relationship with Christ that would be evident through my prayer life. God has used my sister Chrissy to mentor, teach, and guide me.

I remember being invited by her to Bible study. She patiently and lovingly answered my plethora of questions. "Is your church at the start of a new study or in the midst of one? Are they teaching a Beth Moore or Kay Arthur Bible study? What do they teach from?" And so on. Her responses were simple. "My church teaches the Word of God from the Bible. You can come anytime. No, we are not in the middle of a series." The simpler her response, the more I thought she did not understand my questions. See, up until then, I had never attended a Bible study that was not written by someone. I didn't know what it meant or even looked like to conduct a Bible study directly from the Bible itself.

That was just the start of our iron sharpening iron sister in Christ relationship. Chrissy ignites, provokes, and stirs the spirit man in me to go higher, deeper, and wider in everything Jesus. I am so grateful to God for her tenacious, endless press to know Him better and to see His people free to serve Him and live out their predestined plans. She is relentless in her love for God and people. This book is a testament to her surrender to our Abba Father.

In this labor of love that you hold in your hands, Chrissy shares her transition from certain death to life in Jesus Christ. She breaks down complex truths to empower us to overcome the enemy's ploys using our God-given authority and His Word. We are equipped to win! This book shows us how. As we read, we feel her sincere love of Christ and people. We hear her heart's desire for us to know Him and experience His love and abundant life. This book shows us how to use the tools and strategies GOD provided to live the victorious life Jesus

Christ secured for us and receive deliverance from every stronghold, bondage, and the sin that separates us from God. To God be the glory!

I am so grateful to God for His faithfulness in allowing Chrissy to write this book. Iron sharpening iron. May GOD get all the glory as He equips you and takes you from glory to glory.

In Christ's Love,
Nilvia Felipe (Nellie)
Minister, Speaker, Certified Coach of ARIZE Consulting

Who is this author? I'm sure that is the first question that crossed your mind. Let me tell you that through this book, you will be introduced to a young woman who not only loves God but has a personal relationship with Him. This woman of God has shared so much of her personal story with men and women, ministering from a place of relatability. Serving with this woman of God in ministry, you can't help but feel the fire and passion burning inside her. Chrissy Carter is the Co-Pastor of Unity and Love Ministries in Charlotte, NC, and has somehow found the time to channel all that good preaching and teaching into this book that you're holding.

This read will encourage you but not only that; it will cause a self-examination. You need a self-examination; we all do. This read from Pastor Chrissy Carter will step on all ten toes, then lift your head to be sure that you know it's all in love. That's what the love of God does for us, corrects us and gives us instructions on how to proceed after the correction. This can be a magnificent tool for you no matter where you are in your faith walk. New believers can walk through step by step.

Mature believers can walk through step by step. The scripture breakdown is on point, which will make for a great study reference.

You, as the reader, need to know this read is personal, the most effective way to minister, in my opinion. I mean, really, how can a person tell you about anything they have not experienced for themselves. So this lets you in and helps you understand why there is so much passion and desire to share these scriptures and experiences with you. This is not just a book to read: this is life. This is the life that so many are experiencing and have no idea what to do. Well, there's good news now you have help.

Pastor T.J. Austin,
Abundant Life Ministries of Gastonia

Preface

Treatments- 1. managed applications of medicine that's meant to treat a disease. 2. the manner in which someone behaves toward or deals with someone or something. (Merriam-Webster)

These "Love Treatments" are managed applications of the Word of God, prayer, communion, and fasting that are meant to bring healing and deliverance to the reader. Faithfully taking these treatments will result in Christ-like behavior in every area of your life. While reading this book, there will be "divine interruptions" whereby you will need to do a heart check to see what spiritual symptoms are manifesting in your walk. When you identify with those symptoms, repent, renounce those unclean personalities and command them to free you and go into the abyss, never to return. Then you must release and confess the love scriptures over yourself. Take these doses for seven days and watch our Father move on your behalf! If you only knew the resistance and repeated, deliberate attacks that resulted in the loss of chapters and the locking up of devices to keep me from writing this book. That's why I genuinely believe this book will restore families, marriages, churches, and even nations by God's amazing grace.

What is love? The full expression and essence of sacrifice are personified in Christ through the finished work of Calvary. This love has no interruptions, delays, hesitations, or deliberation of expressing what it is assigned to do. It is ever sacrificing and always giving to the point of even death, simply because it never focuses on itself. Love is not selfish, and it never allows anyone to take what it is always willing to give. That's love! Yes, love is beautiful, but there is also a dirty, ugly, and painful side to love! You will see the evidence of love throughout the 66 books of the Bible, and love came for a huge mission to bridge the gap of humankind back to the Father. I love how Love (Jesus) said, "No man takes my life but I freely give it!" And that's exactly what love does, it is always giving and it sacrifices even unto death!

So, this book is meant to illuminate how we as Christians should deliberately strive to be apprehended and held hostage by this type of love. We should live our life for love, through love, and daily receiving Love Treatments to stay built up in our most holy faith. Especially when we consider, faith only works by love! Matthew 24:12 says, *"And because iniquity shall abound, the love of many shall wax cold."* This lets us know that there is a climate that will bring about more and more sin. Well, it's already here but know the conditions will grow worse, and it will cause the hearts of many to grow cold in their love for God for each other.

Do you not see how hate is running rampant and hopelessness is penetrating the hearts of humankind to the point of life-stealing spirit of suicide has caused many to take life into their own hands because love has started waxing cold in man. My desire is for the life-giving love of Jesus Christ, through this book, to collide with your faith and cause a holy fire to ignite like never before. If you, by faith, take your Love Treatments as a daily regiment, purpose to get fully delivered from all the weight of unclean personalities and influences that have hindered you in your love walk. The Bible says some things come by fasting and prayer, so if you want to optimize your love walk, be fully invested, and your life will never be the same!

Introduction

The Process of Love; From Death to Life

Thursday, September 19, 2019, 9:40 PM

I didn't know how dark and destructive my world was until the Lord shook me with a very vivid dream, and it put fear in my heart about how my life would end if I stayed on this wide, destructive road. God showed me that if I didn't slow down and put Him first, I would be in danger of dying prematurely. Still, if that wasn't getting my attention, the encounter I had one evening while sleeping surely did. I had experienced moments when something or someone was holding me down and even felt like I would lose my life if I didn't get up. I tried so hard to open my mouth to pray but couldn't. All I could do was think "Jesus, Jesus, Jesus" until I could fight to speak, and the more I said the name, I could feel the hold of the enemy leaving.

Well, it was more intense on this particular day. Not only did the feeling of being held down reoccur, but I could see a dark, evil spirit moving towards my bed! I knew an assigned enemy was trying to take me out, but I called on the name that was my only lifeline if I was going to get up from this attack! The enemy knew I had made up my mind to come out of the lifestyle that was killing me, and he was retaliating. But oh, the power of the name of Jesus, whereby demons tremble! My Heavenly Father stayed the hands of the spirit of death because again, when I said Jesus, that scary image began to move away, and the enemy that held me down weakened. When I got up this time, things started shifting in a different direction. God had some people assigned to pray for me during this time of my life. The intercession of those people and Jesus worked on my heart, and conviction kicked in. Long story short, He delivered me from death, and my life changed from the "impact" of His love. The main objective of this book is to open up to you by the power of the Holy Spirit and the loyalty of this unconditional love of Jesus Christ.

We must understand this: Our love must go through a process that transitions us from death to life so that we can be productive and fruitful in the Kingdom of God. The door for this process is salvation, the acceptance of Jesus Christ in our hearts, and being baptized in the Holy Spirit, thereby impeaching our sinful old man off the throne by faith. Then, it is the consistent working of the Holy Spirit, who intercedes on behalf of the believer to daily kill off every trace of darkness and death. He does this until the glorious presence of Christ radiates through the life of the Christian. Now, of course, it also takes the yielding of the Christian to let the Holy Spirit lead, for He is our comforter and leads and guides us into all truth.

> *"But when he, the Spirit of truth, comes, he will guide you into all truth. He will not speak on his own; he will only speak what he hears, and he will tell you what is yet to come."* **-John 16:13 NIV**

He is a perfect gentleman and will not force us into change. He waits for the invitation from us to take the lead. Once we ask Him to lead us, He does just that by revealing truths, convicting our hearts, and reminding us what the Father and Jesus have already spoken. Once we commit to letting Him lead, we, in turn, see transformation in all areas of our life little by little, but the depth and hunger for freedom surely opens the door for quick work. Simply put, the relinquishing of man's will along with an intense desire and thirst for God's will is key to moving from dead love to a love that is alive. Praise God!

My mindset says, "My life is no longer my own, but I belong to Him. My desires are no longer driven by my flesh, but I give way to the precious Holy Spirit to lead and guide me into all truth concerning my life's assignment." Our heart's desire must shift from conditional love to unconditional love, that God's glory reveals through us, in the earth.

> *"If we love our brothers and sisters who are believers, it proves that we have passed from death to life. But a person who has no love is still dead."* **-1 John 3:14 NLT**

> *"Jesus replied, "You must love the Lord your God with all your heart, all your soul, and all your mind.' This is the first and greatest commandment. A second is equally important: 'Love your neighbor as yourself.' The entire law and all the demands of the prophets are based on these two commandments."* **-Matthew 22:37-40 NLT**

When we WITHHOLD unconditional love (which is agape love) from those created in the very image and likeness of God, this is evidence that our old man is still controlling our love. It's not reliable to God, you, or anyone else. In other words, it's risky! And that's where I was, in my sin. I was a flight risk until I got tired of the perverted lifestyle that kept me from seeing who I was and seeing the power of Jesus Christ's love for me.

Conditional love is risky because its ground wire is self. Agape love is not only rooted and grounded in Christ alone; it is who Jesus Christ is. This type of love is an eternal asset to the body of Christ! Who wouldn't want their life defined by agape love? Why do we find it so hard to reside in and operate from this type of love? It's because we are dealing with more darkness and death issues than we would like to confess, especially when we understand that confession means to agree with God.

> *"This is the message we heard from Jesus and now declare to you: God is light, and there is no darkness in him at all. So, we are lying if we say we have fellowship with God but go on living in spiritual darkness; we are not practicing the truth. But if we are living in the light, as God is in the light, then we have fellowship with each other, and the blood of Jesus, his Son, cleanses us from all sin. If we claim we have no sin, we are only fooling ourselves and not living in the truth. But if we confess our sins to him, he is faithful and just to forgive us our sins and to cleanse us from all wickedness."*
> **-1 John 1:5-9 NLT**

How many times have you struggled with secret sins that you REFUSE to share with anyone, and won't even confess to God? Many believers barely survive in their walk because they refuse to operate in the truth about where they are. If only we would grasp the value of agape love with soberness, care, and wisdom, we would not take unnecessary hits. We would not find ourselves in continuous self-afflicted situations.

Unfortunately, the enemy uses this very place of self-afflicted trials to hold the believer hostage. Even though they know that God knows all, it's their darkness that hinders their success and undermines the very sure foundation of love, Jesus Christ. If we build on anything else, unquestionably, we will miss the mark. Paul said grace endowed me with the foundation of the very gospel I preach like an expert builder. Indeed, Paul is a credible witness of experiencing the transforming power of Christ's love! He cautions us to be careful about building on what has already been established and confirmed and that there is NO OTHER FOUNDATION! It is the very foundation of agape love that supports our Christian life.

> *"Because of God's grace to me, I have laid the foundation like an expert builder. Now others are building on it. But whoever is building on this foundation must be very careful. For no one can lay any foundation other*

than the one we already have—Jesus Christ." **-1 Corinthians 3:10-11 NLT**

Many Christians and churchgoers are oppressed by traditions, religion, porn, perversion, homosexuality, lesbianism, rage, depression, jealousy, unforgiveness, fear, stress, anxiety, immorality, soul-ties, condemnation, unbelief, addictions, heresies, paranoia, schizophrenia, and other dark strongholds. Their lives are filled with constant pain, depression, emotional and physical attacks on their bodies, anger, and constantly holding onto offenses while justifying their actions. The truth is a breach has penetrated and, in some ways, obstructed the foundation. The enemy's deception is to keep this truth hidden. One of his ploys against the Christian is to keep them from seeing how unprepared they are against his tactics, all the while keeping them distracted with the cares of this world. I love this quote and believe it brings imagery to our condition in the Church: *"War is a terrible thing. But if you're going to get into it, you've got to get into it all the way."* General Dwight Eisenhower

Many Christians are defeated in their Christian lives because they are not seriously engaged in the call to warfare. J. C. Ryle saw this in the 19th century and wrote, "*The saddest symptom about many so-called Christians is the utter absence of anything like conflict and fight in their Christianity."* (*Soldiers and Trumpeters*, Home Truths [Triangle Press], 1:90) He went on to say that they go through the motions of attending religious services each week. *"But of the great spiritual warfare, --its watchings and struggling, its agonies and anxieties, its battles and contests,--of all this they appear to know nothing at all."*

It's undeniable that there is tremendous suffering in the Church when Christians stop at salvation and neglect to follow through to become true disciples of Jesus Christ. Love and truth fuel true discipleship, and there is no sustainability apart from it. We must know there is a war waging against the unconditional love of Christ.

Lack of commitment to the call and refusal to go all the way into the sanctification process is one of the many breach areas of the Christian foundation. Just use your spiritual imagination for a moment and picture someone halfway committed to boarding an aircraft to get to the other side of the world. It's the refusal to be all in that keeps them from boarding the plane. Although they have a mission to accomplish, it's an incomplete mission because the commitment is not greater than appeasing and nurturing their fears. Anything can come between completing the assignment (the very purpose of God)! It is where many believers fail. We half commit to the kingdom of God but want all the benefits, as if we are active, full-time servants. The focus for too many Christians zooms in on the hand of God, the things He can do, while disobedience, noncompliance, and being unmanageable persist. But these, my brothers and sisters, are due to dark areas we must recognize and have the determination to break free!

There must be a holy desire to know Him in the fellowship of His suffering first because this is where we see love in its fullness. The very fact that He willingly died in our place reveals His unconditional love for all of humanity. But when will we voluntarily surrender our lives over for His Glory?

Please hear me when I say I do not speak these things in any way to look down on the person(s) that find themselves in any of these places. I most certainly can identify with some of these areas. There are areas that God has graced me to walk in victory, and there are areas I've significantly failed, but even then, the failures served a purpose. It allowed me to experience the relentlessness of Christ's love for me. I'm sure every reader has something operating in their life or has experienced something that you were and or are a prisoner to right now. It's to that very place that I want to appeal. Unconditional love is vital for every deliverance and sustained deliverance. The agape love covers sin, and this love alone benefits the recipient with sure results.

Question? Have you ever experienced a person with the mindset that things in their life wouldn't be so bad if other people would do their part? If other people had been on their posts, my life wouldn't be so bad. If this deception didn't transpire, my life wouldn't be this way. If a relative didn't molest me, I wouldn't be on guard, and it would be easier to forgive. I wouldn't be this way if my father did not abandon me. These areas are deceptive strategies and the operation of darkness attempting to justify why you have every right to place conditions on your love. If we do not uproot these sections, the issues of life will not be favorable. Our love determines how we handle trials and testing, which is the basic training for purpose! Blame shifting and fault finding keep a person bound.

As you read further, I hope that the Holy Spirit will bring conviction, not condemnation, to everyone imprisoned by these oppressions, snares, and yokes of bondage. I hope those dead areas are resurrected and come alive! For the unconditional love of Christ to be manifested fully in our life, we must without hesitation lay hold to the truth. The Word of God is our sure foundation on which we build, and if we allow issues to remain or persist in our hearts, we will still be operating from a dark place. It's time for us to own our portion and start working from there because this is the only way to encounter life more abundantly. The Holy Spirit's working power through revelation illuminates how the enemy has used blind spots to keep us from seeing the truth and what that truth is. We are a liability to the kingdom of God because our love is risky! It's risky because our self is still in the driver's seat. These chapters have an assignment to pull every reader to a sound and reliable place in their relationship with Jesus. Thus, making them a true asset for Our Heavenly Father and releasing His glory on us on Earth!!

My heart desires to persuade every reader to live as sons of God, whose mission is to become love agents for God's Kingdom. These daily love treatments will bring healing and deliverance to your very soul with the condition you take them daily.

Remember that this is the only way you and I can advance the Kingdom through effective evangelism, prophetic services, revivals that shake our cities, and signs and wonders following. I believe that God has graced your life to be a sure reflection of His love in the Earth!

~Pastor Chrissy Darlene Carter

Chapter 1

The Unrealized, Inexhaustible Riches and Wealth of Christ's Love

"I pray that out of His glorious riches He may strengthen you with power through His Holy Spirit in your inner being, so that Christ may dwell in your hearts through faith. And I pray that you, being rooted and established in love, may have power, together with all the Lord's Holy people, to grasp how wide and long and high and deep is the love of Christ." **-Ephesians 3: 16-18 (NIV)**

Unrealized- Not brought to conscious awareness: Not understood

Inexhaustible- (Of an amount or supply of something) unable to be used up because existing in abundance.

When I look around our country and see all the problems we face, it further confirms we are living in the last days. We're dealing with a pandemic, hate crimes, addictions, depression, mental health issues, homes still divided, corruption on every level, pseudo-Christians, prostitution, human trafficking, wars and rumors of wars, the spirit of darkness rearing its head through the COVID-19 virus, economic decline, fires, floods, trouble in the White House, and earthquakes in various places. It is a spiritual indicator that we are closer to Christ's return than when we first believed.

Jesus said these would be the beginning of birth pains in Matthew 24:8, but when Paul refers to the last days in the NIV translation, he starts with "but mark this." These three words command the hearer's attention and urge the believer to take action. He then shares the climate change that would impact our society in a manner that could be labeled "the perfect storm." This storm reveals the condition of man's heart. Sadly, we see division, pride, selfishness, perversion, disobedience, and people denying the very power of God but drawing to forms of godliness, loving the pleasures of this world rather than loving God! It is a very unhealthy and deadly place for anyone that desires real life.

Remember, this warning is for the church. Please take a look around us right now and carefully do a personal check off of events, conditions, and the descriptive list of both Jesus and Paul. It's as if you can see the hand of the Father, Himself checking the boxes of each description. Therefore, it would be wise for us to listen to the scriptures and press into His presence to seek revelation and direction on proceeding in such a critical and treacherous climate. So, take a moment and read the scriptures below and soberly assess where you are in these last and perilous days.

> *But mark this: There Will be terrible times in the last days. People will be lovers of themselves, lovers of money, boastful, proud, abusive, disobedient to their parents, ungrateful, unholy, without love, unforgiving, slanderous, without self-control, brutal, not lovers of the good, treacherous, rash, conceited, lovers of pleasure rather than lovers of God- having a form of godliness but denying its power. Have nothing to do with such people.* **-2 Timothy 3:1- 5 NIV**

> *Later, Jesus sat on the Mount of Olives. His disciples came to him privately and said, "Tell us, when will all this happen? What sign will signal your return and the end of the world?" Jesus told them, "Don't let anyone mislead you, for many will come in my name, claiming, 'I am the Messiah.' They will deceive many. And you will hear of wars and threats of wars, but don't panic. Yes, these things must take place, but the end won't follow*

> *immediately. Nation will go to war against nation, and kingdom against kingdom. There will be famines and earthquakes in many parts of the world. But all this is only the first of the birth pains, with more to come.* - **Matthew 24:3-8 NLT**

When we read the words of Jesus, we see that we are not in those real, life-threatening labor pains right now, but we are at the beginning of birth pains. For the mothers who have experienced pregnancy, we know that nature must take its course when the actual labor pains kick in, and it's time to deliver! But Jesus gives a keyword to explain this particular time we live in right now, beginning. We know that when we are at the beginning of a thing, that means it's just getting started. Like birth pains, we mothers have experienced the warm-up contractions called the Braxton Hicks that usually occur during our second trimester. Likewise, these are just the beginning of difficult times that will only get worse with time. The closer the delivery date, the longer and stronger the birth pains (contractions).

Please understand, Jesus said these things must happen, but how should the believer operate during these times? I believe the only wise way to respond is in soberness, watchfulness, maintaining constant prayer, and communion with the Father while displaying the love that covers a multitude of sins. It is sure to position the believer to be prepared for what's next and is what Jesus revealed to His disciples to ensure their proper preparation.

A huge portion of this preparation comes when we, the church, are clear-headed about the great exchange that took place on Calvary and the fullness of our inheritance. If only we could understand the wealth we possess on the inside. The Holy Spirit is not only our deposit guaranteeing what is to come, but right now, at this moment, we have access to a love bank! Hallelujah Jesus!

> *Now it is God who makes both us and you stand firm in Christ. He anointed us, set his seal of ownership on us, and put his spirit in our hearts as a deposit, guaranteeing what is to come.* **-2 Corinthians 1:21-22 NIV**

One thing we must lay hold of during these times is the unrealized, inexhaustible riches of God's favor, faithfulness, and love for His church (the bride of Christ). The word says, "For God so loved the world that He gave His only begotten Son," (John 3:16 NIV) meaning no one is exempt from the impact of this love. It's about entering into the "whosoever will let them come" invitation.

The Father needs His sons watching, praying and there must be a sober awareness of how great His love is towards humanity. This love is never on backorder, out of stock, unreachable, unavailable, unattainable, or closed off to anyone. It can never be depleted or exhausted. The real question is, how sober are we about the resources we have access to, and do we have a genuine desire to explore this love? Let's go even further. It's the grace of God that opens us up to the true source of love, so why would we not operate in these special graces that are right at our fingertips? Keep in mind these are special privileges that came with the "Finished Work of Calvary Package Plan," like the operation and power of the Holy Spirit who lives in us. The powers of confession, repentance, righteousness now conferred upon our life, the armor of God, fasting, the blood of the Lamb, the Word of God, the name of Jesus, and prayer are endless love extended to us!

One may look at this package plan and wonder what does the blood have to do with anything? Well, it washed our sins away. It's the cleansing agent that sanctifies and a healing agent, but also a protection for your very life. His shed blood alone is evidence of His great love for all humanity. We see how the blood of lambs, rams and goats were placed on the doorpost of Gods people, protecting them from the death angel but the blood of Jesus Christ protects those who believe far more than we can ever think or imagine.

Even as I lay hold to this truth, it prompts a desire to pray for the reader at this very moment. So, let's touch and agree.

> Father, in the name of Jesus, lead and guide us into all truth as it pertains to this love you are revealing to us, even in the difficult times we see today. We ask that you search us and know us and if there be anything contrary to Your will, lead us in an everlasting way. Help us to lose sight of what we have thought love to be by the power of your Holy Spirit. Lord, reveal every trace of fear, doubt, pride, unforgiveness, or anything we have placed before You, including our spouses or children. Please deliver us and divinely help us to prioritize those areas. You commanded us to have no other gods before You. The cares of this world can easily throw us off task and cause us to zoom in on the blessings rather than the giver of the blessings. Please have mercy on us, Father. Do not charge it not to our account. Create in us a clean heart and renew a right spirit in us. Let the words of our mouths and the meditation of our hearts be acceptable in Your sight. We believe by faith that You will transform us from the inside out for your glory! Holy Spirit, please lead and guide us into all truth. We pray for a pliable and supple heart that will lay hold to the vastness of Your love for us. Teach us to number our days upon earth so that we do not squander any time on mindless distractions. Please help us walk in Your unconditional love daily. We believe it and receive it, in Jesus' name! Amen!

So now, we must understand that desire is vital for impact, productivity, and effectiveness in any assignment or task. The reason desire is a must is that we won't squander what we have but steward instead. Why would the Father make so much of Himself available to us if He didn't want us to pursue, long for, and search Him out? Listen, our Father is not wasteful, nor will He force men to search for Him. Still, He will allow the master that man chooses to have his way until humanity realizes how much we need Him. When we recognize the times we live in and consider the kingdom assignment ahead of us, it will behoove us to be deliberate in our love. You see, love stands in any condition and should be the answer we pursue, the love of Christ. Matthew 6:24 tells us man can't serve two masters. He would love one but hate the other. Man cannot serve love (Christ) and mammon (material riches). We must choose before we can come close to realizing the inexhaustible riches and wealth in Jesus Christ.

Think about the many opportunities you had to draw closer to God but didn't? Think about how many excuses you came up with to justify your lack of desire. We make time for the things we truly desire. So, if our desires have landed us in places, with people and seeking out material things, more than the face of God, we will never encounter the fullness of Christ's love for us. Instead, it will cause us to stray in our relationship with Him.

I believe the Apostle Paul understood the importance of being fully immersed, rooted, and established in the love of Jesus and how far that love would travel. It is evident when we have an understanding of Paul's story.

My question for you is, "Do you really understand the fullness of this powerful love in all of its many sacrifices?" Once you are properly rooted and grounded in this love, then you can operate in it with the assurance of authority and power! The Greek word for this authority is exousia, which expresses both freedom and legal rights. The Bible uses it in numerous ways.

So, let's take a closer look at what this means. The enemy knows if he can hinder the unconditional love of Christ from flowing through us, it impedes and depletes our freedom and legal rights to operate as a Kingdom citizen. That means that the enemy's strategies can lessen our reach to penetrate and impact a dying world. Satan knows that if he devalues the desire to operate in this perfect love, humankind won't seize the opportunity to yield to the Holy Spirit.

Simply put, the devil is after your love! He has launched an all-out attack that's aimed directly at the perfect love in you! He runs interference daily, bringing distractions, offenses, love of money, idols, and fear. You may think having unconditional love is a tall order. You are right because, honestly, our love won't make the cut. We often give way to our soul, the very part of us that's still in agreement with our flesh. But, listen, all the Father wants us to do is yield our members and our soul to the leading of the Holy Spirit. We won't get talking back in disagreement from our spirit man because from the moment we truly accepted Christ as Lord and Savior; it's in harmony with the Holy Spirit. The resistance comes from our soul (mind, will, and emotions). It's the Holy Spirit and our spirit man working together to win our soul over for service.

As sons of God, service is essential. The only way we can correctly position ourselves to serve is by yielding. The word yield in Greek is Eiko, which means submission, give way, to imitate the One in authority, to comply with, and "to make less, to be conquered by One." (Bible Hub) Okay, now let's pull this all together, so it gives more insight. We don't have to take on the burden of trying to meet the mark with our love. All we need to do is submit, give way, imitate the one in authority, and comply with Him by making ourselves less because the power of His love has conquered us. Just let the Holy Spirit love through you by being a channel of love. Do you see the endless riches and wealth wrapped up in His love?

When looking at the virtues in 1 Corinthians 13:13, three things will last forever, faith, hope, and love, and the greatest of these is love. Paul does something for us in this chapter. He removes man's excuse to hide behind works, gifts, and kind acts. He says in 1 Corinthians 13: 1-3 NIV, *"If I speak in the tongues of men and of angels, but have not love, I am only a resounding gong or a clanging cymbal. If I have the gift of prophecy and can fathom all mysteries and all knowledge, and if I have a faith that can move mountains, but do not have love, I am nothing."* In Galatians 5:6, we learn that to live in Christ Jesus is to have faith expressed through love. We should not expect to stand firm in the middle of a pandemic when our love is not as it should be. This heart condition will have us operating in one of these many areas Paul describes in 2 Timothy 3:1-5.

Remember, this list describes society, the climate, and the offensive posture of man. But it could also describe us if we are not in the right place with our love. So, brothers and sisters, our highest and our greatest desire should be to have a divine revelation of the fullness of this love. Why does Jesus spend so much time during his earthly ministry, demonstrating the power of healing and deliverance which comes through love? It would be foolish to see Jesus showing something of this magnitude and not believe He wants us to imitate His actions.

Everything He did was relevant and purposeful. It had an assignment then, and it has an assignment now. Know that your love's assignment will surely fulfill its mission when you relinquish your own will for the will of the Holy Spirit. The work that Jesus centered His mission on and continues to center His love around is John 3:16. His desire for humankind is to pick up where He left off in His earthly ministry. It is why we must seek and find out everything we can about this unrestricted, unbounded love, supremely for the sake of completing the assignment that Jesus gave us in Matthew 28:16-20.

Let's read and meditate on these two hallmark scriptures.

> *"For God so loved the world, that he gave his only begotten Son, that whosoever believeth in him should not perish, but have everlasting life."*
> **John 3:16 KJV**

> *"Then the eleven disciples left for Galilee, going to the mountain where Jesus had told them to go. When they saw him, they worshiped him—but some of them doubted! Jesus came and told his disciples, "I have been given all authority in heaven and on earth. Therefore, go and make disciples of all the nations, baptizing them in the name of the Father and the Son and the Holy Spirit. Teach these new disciples to obey all the commands I have given you. And be sure of this: I am with you always, even to the end of the age."*
> **Matthew 28:16-20 NLT**

It's one thing to give or sacrifice something you have more of, but when your demonstration of love is on the level of our Heavenly Father, it is an isolated case. This type of love and giving has never been duplicated. It never can be because Jesus was and is the only one of His kind, the perfect son in every sense of perfection! He knew NO SIN and became our scapegoat so that we are not eternally separated from our Father.

The Father gives with a currency of love, on a level that humanity is still trying to perceive, receive and embrace. But take a look at what Jesus does with His disciples on their last meeting. He gives His sons an assignment because He has nurtured, taught, and mentored them, and now is the time for them to receive their Apostolic Commission. It takes place in an area they have met together before. All twelve do not show up at the ceremony, only the ones that completed basic training. Jesus reminds them that He has all authority and power given to Him over the heavens and the earth. Therefore, as Commander and Chief, He lets them know that He can send them wherever He pleases.

> "All dominates Matthew 28:18-20 and ties these verses together: all authority, all nations, all things, all days." (Enduring Word Commentary, www.enduringword.com)

> "Power in the hands of some people is dangerous but in the Hands of Christ is blessed. Oh, let Him have all the power! Let Him do what He will with it, for He cannot will anything but that which is right, and just, and true, and good." (Enduring Word Commentary, www.enduringword.com)

Jesus is commanding them to go, and He has every right to do so. The Father gave, so now He must receive a great return on His investment. He handled man's death issue by paying the huge debt with His Son's blood, and He expects full payment by using the life of humankind for His Glory! Hallelujah, Lord Jesus!! What a very tall order Lord, asking imperfect men to take on such a monumental task, especially when You still see the flaws. Lord, You know we are still trying to work through some of these crazy mistakes we made. Peter, with his quick temper and denial of who you are, Thomas, the doubter, and James and John offended, wanting to call down fire from Heaven. Yet, the Lord is saying, "Go therefore and make disciples of all the nations."

Listen, brothers and sisters, love will send you to places you don't think you are qualified to handle, yet you still have the command to go. But be assured you are not going alone. The Lord is with you on this journey, and everything Jesus willingly did on the Earth, He will do through your life. It's time for the body of Christ to hunger for the eyes of her understanding, to be open for the sake of soberly realizing the fullness of this inexhaustible, eternal love.

Chapter 2

Love Sees a Return from Its Investment

"Agape love is never hindered by the unknown; its assignment is to complete its mission to break the stronghold of fear! This love is thorough (complete concerning every detail, not superficial or partial)." - **Chrissy D. Carter**

We allow what we do not know to hinder our commitment to say yes to the call of love and willingly be the love our neighbors need. God commands us to love, and our response to issues, disappointments, people used by the enemy and the unknown is to be the love that shows up or, better yet, the love that people find. See, the thing about love is that it does not need guard rails or manufactured protective gear where we fear being vulnerable versus being the agent of love. There is a price (cost) for loving. I heard my husband give that same message to one of our daughters in the faith because she had lost a loved one. He shared that when we lose someone close to us, it's a part of the price we pay for loving, but there is a grace to get through it.

So, my heart's desire for you is to experience and know the power of Christ's love. His love should in no way cause us to be guarded. Instead, it should place a desire in us to love harder and a determination to let the love of the Holy Spirit win in us every time. I want to encourage you to be strong and courageous with this love! Don't allow your past pain to lead you but let love take the lead. The Lord spoke to me and said, "Love and pain got married over two thousand years ago, and they are not getting a divorce." Your victory is determined by which one is leading. It's when we deliberately yield to love that sets us up for the win. Hallelujah, Lord Jesus, for the victory!

Just because you don't have all the details or a complete view of what lies ahead doesn't excuse you from the assignment to bear up under the weight of love so you can bear all things. So let me explain further what it means to bear up. In Greek, anéxomai (aná, "up/completing a process" and exō, "to have") means properly, "still bearing up," even after going through the needed sequence (course of action); to forbear. For the believer, "staying up" means living out God's works in faith.

We have a mandate to live out the faith that the Father built inside of us. To do that, we must rid ourselves of all the distractions and soberly guard against the satanic traps and ploys of the enemy. There is another significant enemy we must beware of, and that's the inner-me that's full of excuses. All of these things and more will hi-jack your desire to know the power of agape love more intimately. Why is that? It's because, after the fall of man, we settled for the love that keeps us in control rather than the love that requires us to die! We don't want to die because we believe we know what's best for us, but the burden of proof is in the garden. Adam and Eve took away that excuse and left all of humanity with a destructive mess.

My brothers and sisters, this is all the more reason to freely give up your life as you know it in exchange for a life that's hidden in Christ. When you decide that it's in Him that you live, move, and have your being, everything changes. Your response won't be the same. You won't perceive things through the lens of your old man, and you won't entertain the dead things, the worldly things that hold you, hence causing you to forfeit freedom in Christ Jesus.

Christ's love is no lightweight, play-play type of love that has all kinds of conditions attached. Instead, His love is likened to the heaviest sort of weight that ever existed. For every assignment it's called to, nothing can move it from fulfilling its mission. So, if we are to bear up under the weight of this type of love, it won't allow you to commit partially. It is when intense endurance kicks in to say, "Not my will but thy will be done!" This bearing up takes patience and persistence if your desired end is to love unconditionally. To bear all things, we must realize that this word bear also means to cover.

Let's examine the scriptures and hear what the Apostle Paul says by the Spirit of the Lord. In the following verse, charity is another word for love.

> *"Charity suffereth long, and is kind; charity envieth not; charity vaunteth not itself, is not puffed up, Doth not behave itself unseemly, seeketh not her own, is not easily provoked, thinketh no evil; Rejoiceth not in iniquity, but rejoiceth in the truth; Beareth all things, believeth all things, hopeth all things, endureth all things."* **-1 Corinthians 13:4-7 (KJV)**

Love bears all things is not suggestive, and it's not optional. It is the Spirit of God operating through the life of a believer to bear, not just a few things but all things. You may ask the question, how is that possible? Simply put, the Greater One in you will accomplish the task, but you must first be willing to deny yourself and then pick up your cross. Let me take it further, die to yourself and allow the Holy Spirit to live through you daily. He will endow the believer to bear all things. Yes, this pushes and pressures us to mature in this authentic love that only has eyes for the mission rather than the convenience of man's focus on excuses. God must have complete cooperation from the church to go deeper in her love for Him, the people we serve alongside (brothers and sisters in the faith), and also for a dying world! Hallelujah! I believe this is an honor and privilege for the church even to have access to something this powerful but oh how we have diminished this one word. We have made common the powerful action that broke our chains of bondage, our yokes of depression, and the strongholds of the devil. Sadly, we have played, flirted, and even become a host for the very enemy of this love. Father, have mercy on us and forgive us for our selfishness, shortsightedness, and spiritual infidelity against You.

The word bear in 1 Corinthians 13 also translates as cover, to cover all. 1 Peter 4:8 NKJV says, *"And above all things have fervent love for one another, for 'love will cover a multitude of sins."* Our love will never make the cut, but the great love of Christ in us will always cover a multitude of sins.

The other thing we must remember is it's not our love to withhold. Jesus died for His love to be expressed in the Earth! Who are we to mishandle, misrepresent and withhold this love? Meditate on this question for a moment and begin to ask the Lord to reveal every dark place in your heart that's not like Him, and He will. Once He reveals these areas, begin to repent and then renounce them. When you renounce them, you are taking away the legal right of the enemy to live in your body (which is the temple of the Lord). It was never intended for satanic habitation. On the contrary, our temples celebrate the most incredible celebration of all times, the life of Christ in us! God never wanted demons to have access to you, but the fall of Adam and Eve opened this door.

Your body is a dwelling place for the Holy Spirit and not unclean squatters. Everything that God the Father would ever do to impact the earth, His desire has always been to do it through us. So likewise, God in us, the precious Holy Spirit in us, causes the kingdom of heaven to impact the earth. When we are operating in the unconditional love of Jesus Christ, there is no stopping this significant impact!

"Don't you realize that your body is the temple of the Holy Spirit, who

lives in you and was given to you by God? You do not belong to yourself, for God bought you with a high price. So you must honor God with your body." **-1 Corinthians 6:19-20 NLT**

Renounce- To declare against; to reject or decline formally; to refuse to own or acknowledge as belonging to one; to disclaim; as, to renounce a title to land or to a throne. To cast off or reject deliberately; to disown; to dismiss; to forswear. (www.biblehub.com)

Squatter- a person who unlawfully occupies an uninhabited building or unused land; a settler with no legal title to the land occupied, typically one on land not yet allocated by a government. (Oxford Languages)

Have you ever wondered why it took you so long to come to Christ? Why did you choose to go through so much defeat, low living, fear, anger, promiscuity, and darkness? It's because you were not wrestling against your flesh, but there was an illegal entry. Whatever you were big and bad enough to do, the spiritual squatters influenced it. Don't let anyone deceive you into thinking that you don't deal with demons or that was only for the Bible days. Not true! We all are dealing with influences from the kingdom of darkness in one way or another. It's about how honest you will be in those dealings. It's about how transparent you will be about where you are and what you're dealing with.

The Bible speaks loudly about what we don't wrestle with, flesh and blood. Then it gives specifics about what we wrestle with, rulers of darkness, powers, spiritual wickedness, and principalities in high places. The Bible also tells us to put on the whole armor of God because the weapons of our warfare are not carnal but mighty through God to the pulling down of strongholds! It's time for us to resist the enemy that's after our love!

"For we are not fighting against flesh-and-blood enemies, but against evil

rulers and authorities of the unseen world, against mighty powers in this dark world, and against evil spirits in the heavenly places. Therefore, put on every piece of God's armor so you will be able to resist the enemy in the time of evil. Then after the battle you will still be standing firm." **-Ephesians 6:12-13 (NLT)**

"(For the weapons of our warfare are not carnal, but mighty through God to the pulling down of strong holds;) Casting down imaginations, and every high thing that exalteth itself against the knowledge of God, and bringing into captivity every thought to the obedience of Christ; And having in us a readiness to revenge all disobedience, when your obedience is fulfilled." **-2 Corinthians 10:4-6 (KJV)**

"Submit yourselves therefore to God. Resist the devil, and he will flee from you." **-James 4:7 (KJV)**

The enemy's job is to keep the church from operating in her daily dose of love that drips from Calvary's Cross. His assignment is to steal, kill and destroy the lives of God's children. What you must understand is that you are not reading this book by chance. God has divinely positioned you to see better so you can love better, which in turn will posture you to live better! Hallelujah, Lord Jesus! Oh, if we would but trust His providential hand in our life to the point where no matter where we find ourselves, we know He is at work in us even when we don't have a clue about what's going on. We must purpose to decree today that no matter how I feel, God's plan for our life is greater than our feelings. The key is to lay hold to His never-ending love for us because that's our beginning point of reference. He first loved me; therefore, I must lay hold to this love and let it work for me, in me and then ooze out of me for His glory!

If we would realize the many missed opportunities, we have forfeited because we refused to yield and let love win. Why do we talk ourselves out of the very thing that has the most incredible power on the Earth?

Why do we make excuses for our half-hearted behavior? I believe it has a lot to do with false adaptations that keep us comfortable in the familiar. If we break it down further, our old man has the legal right to have a say still and remain as a live-in tenant in this new walk with Jesus Christ. Ephesians 4:20-24 (NKJV) instructs us, *"But you have not so learned Christ, if indeed you have heard Him and have been taught by Him, as the truth is in Jesus: that you put off, concerning your former conduct, the old man which grows corrupt according to the deceitful lusts, and be renewed in the spirit of your mind, and that you put on the new man which was created according to God, in true righteousness and holiness."*

There are three critical instructions where we, the church, have dropped the ball. First, we refused to put off our old man, be renewed in the spirit of our mind, and put on the new man. Second, suppose we don't quickly address the obvious and meet the requirements. In that case, we will be in danger of continuing to operate in the form of godliness and deny the very power that could save a nation. The third danger here is that anyone operating from this place stays offended or intimidated by something or someone. That alone is the hindrance to serving in the love of Christ.

You see, it's only after a person has counted the cost of following Christ and experienced the true vastness of His riches in mercy that life takes on an entirely new meaning. It's the one forgiven the most, who can love the most and the hardest because Christ planted an eternal seed in their life (Luke 7:36-50). Oh yes, when the seed of truth downloads on a Damascus Road experience, all of the mess, wrongs, persecution, and the taking of men's lives flash right before your eyes. A great light shines and exposes everything you ever did. Still, with merciful discipline, love looks beyond the faults and zooms into His purpose for your life. It is where Saul, who transformed into the Apostle Paul, found himself. He was face to face with great light, the very light that John speaks about in John 1:5 (NIV), *"The light shines in the darkness and the darkness has not overcome it."*

So now Saul has just met his match, as the Lord meets him on His turf and His terms. This experience had to be on this level, considering the resume of this madman Saul. The very one who is having the church, that Love died for, persecuted and killed. Note, there was something in operation inside of Saul that would serve as a vital attribute for the calling and purpose of his life, his respect for authority. He did not pursue the believers of the Way without permission from the high priest, believing he was doing good work for the Lord. After all, he was a young, educated man of the law.

Can you see the boldness of Saul to go so hard pursuing something he was really in the dark about? How many people leave their purpose on the shelf of life untouched because they don't know how things will turn out? They are deceived into thinking they must be in control. Before his experience with Christ, Saul is in a unique situation. He is well educated and regards handling even his persecution towards the church in an orderly fashion, considering he gets permission before going into this furious, persecution mode. We must see the value of this character trait and his passion. But, of course, he is used by the enemy to kick against the will of God. Saul not knowing he is on the wrong side isn't an issue for love because love is in hot pursuit, coming straight for him!

In this chapter, you will see how the love of Christ is never hindered by what man is not privy to. It doesn't matter that you don't know the fullness of your purpose. It doesn't matter if you are still praying for wayward children who don't know about their assignment in the Body of Christ. Trust that the love of Jesus Christ isn't hindered by the things you can't see! Hallelujah, Lord Jesus! Oh, that deserves a praise break right there! We can testify about this truth because we didn't have a clue as to how Jesus was going to use us. But it didn't stop love from covering us, protecting us, and throwing us a lifeline! Glory to God for His sovereignty!

When God spoke those words to me, "Love is never hindered by the unknown," I didn't understand the simplicity of the message. You know how we can try and take a message somewhere and get all deep. Well, the Lord took me back to preschool. He said, "It's not that deep Chrissy. That's when I do My best work, when you're in the blind." In other words, it's not uncovered or revealed because revelation has an appointed time. So, it was now time for Saul to have an encounter with the lover of his soul!

One may attempt to question the love of God for the church due to the lives taken, but we sometimes overlook the real enemy behind the scenes, and we give him a pass. We know the devil never fights fair, and he is the author of confusion, but more so, he comes to steal, kill and destroy. It is indisputable that the spirit of religion, persecution, and murder was having a field day with Saul but look at how love comes to the rescue! We must see about love is that He sees what we can't see, and it's always about Him getting a great return on His investment. Love is farsighted or rather all-seeing and long-suffering. A sober assessment of the life of Paul after his conversion reveals that God knew what type of return He would get from the apostle's life.

Look at how the Lord uses a "grace fall" for His glory but Paul's purpose. Why do I call it a "grace fall"? First, because it was a favor he didn't deserve. It was a fall that positioned him for the unrealized, inexhaustible riches of Christ's love. Now Saul is open to some spiritual truths. We also see the infinite wisdom of God presenting Himself in a manner that would quickly humble and even paralyze Saul. But more importantly, it would serve as a defining moment that would simultaneously bring about a name change and a character change.

He uses His light to overcome and overpower the darkness in Saul. The glory of this great light also blinds him physically enlightens him spiritually for his assignment. Here he comes face to face with the light that lights the heart of all men, the light of truth Himself. This encounter reveals the power of light and truth that came from Jesus. He has divinely established what would be the best approach to reach Saul and forever impact his life. That's why we cannot step in the way of God by attempting to prejudge a situation or people. It is God who decides how He will draw the unbelievers into His kingdom and restore the backslider. We do not know the method the Lord will use, but we know He will draw from love and kindness. He laces even His judgment with love.

Remember, this is not just a regular interruption in Saul's day but a divine interruption that reveals his current state. Jesus asked Saul why he was persecuting Him? He responded, "It's hard to kick against the goads." An ox goad is a sharp stick used to poke or prod the cattle. So, Jesus revealed to Saul that he was only hurting himself every time he kicked against His truth. Every time he kicked against love, he was only harming himself. God uses a method that Saul had not experienced to unveil his destiny in Christ Jesus. Isn't it amazing how the Lord poses a simple question to bring Saul's attention to the problem he has caused himself and the church? He helps Saul to see that what he intended for the church was utterly against the Lord. It is a spiritual truth that can help us to handle people differently. Especially when we realize how we treat our brother or sister in Christ, it is just like doing it to the Lord! Jesus had already spoken about this in Matthew 25:40 (NLT), *"And the King will say, I tell you the truth, when you did it to one of the least of these my brothers and sisters, you were doing it to me!"*

We, the church, must realize that how we mistreat people is a sin against God. Honestly, God could have taken this time to read all of Saul's mail with much anger. But, instead, love asked a question, which in turn inspired Saul to ask, "Who are You Lord?" It was his first supernatural encounter with Jesus, the turning point of a revolutionary love pursuit.

Please don't allow fear or frustration to distract or hold hostage your faith in God for the salvation of your spouse, children, or family members no matter their age because Love is not hindered by the unknown. He shows up just in the nick of time on a Damascus Road. The power of this love is so great that its light penetrates deep. It's quick, powerful, and sharper than any two-edged sword, piercing to divide soul, spirit, joints, and marrow asunder. It discerns the thoughts and intents of the heart. And hear me, nothing in creation can hide from love, but everything is open, exposed, and naked. (Hebrews 4:12- 13)

When love shows up in Word form or glory mode, a transformation will take place. Please know there is no limit to the power of love, and there is no area in your life that is so messed up it can't be fixed. We must remember love already knows everything there is to know about you, and He still hasn't changed His mind about using you! Think about it. In everybody else's mind, Saul was their enemy and a threat to their peace. They wanted nothing to do with him. I'm sure some people wanted him dead, but love takes an entirely different approach. Love says, "I'm going to let my love overpower you and then blind you!" The love Saul was kicking against has now apprehended him! I don't know about you, but I'm so grateful that love won't give up on me, even when I'm in the dark about the chapters in my life. We must come to a mutual agreement that if we are on the wrong side of God's will, love can show up unexpectedly on any page in our life's story.

Sometimes we allow fear of the unknown to keep us running. Therefore, I want to encourage you in the Lord by sharing Proverbs 3:5-6 NKJV, *"Trust in the Lord with all your heart, lean not to your own understanding but in all of your ways acknowledge Him (Love) and He (Love) shall direct your path."*

Chapter 3

Turn On the Light

"The one who is the true light, who gives light to everyone, was coming into the world." **-John 1:9 (NLT)**

"The revelation of Your words brings light and gives understanding to the inexperienced." **-Psalms 119:130 (CSB)**

Our nation is in dire need of light. Unfortunately, so many things manifest themselves in the form of darkness and have already become normal to the church. Sadly, we tend to handle the truth and love of Christ like a light switch we can flip off and on as we feel. You must know that there are two kinds of kingdoms fighting for a position in the heart of man, and we must choose from which place we are going to operate. God, our Father, created everything, and He represents the kingdom of light while Satan represents the kingdom of darkness. Everything that represents the truth comes from the kingdom of light, and everything that represents a lie comes from the kingdom of darkness.

We are still not operating to the total capacity that God has graced us to operate in due to the absence of light in our personal lives. Jesus is this true light, and He gives light to everyone. But why are we not seeing clearly? Undoubtedly, the problem is not with the true light, and it will never be with Him. So that means we (the church) are the holdup.

John 1:10-12 NLT speaks of Jesus being the true light coming into the world, but they didn't recognize Him. So he went to His own, and they rejected Him. However, it didn't stop the light from moving. In verse 12, grace kicked in and said, *"But to all who received and accepted him, he gave the right to become the children of God."*

So, let's look at this closer. Light has come into the world, but it does not recognize the light. The word world in Greek is Kosmos, often used to refer to the fallen, sinful system of thinking. It is the worldly mindset that rejects God, His knowledge, and His word. They love darkness rather than the light that brought truth because their hearts are evil. The word recognize in Greek is epiginosko, to know exactly or to know through personal relationship; realized, aware.

Man's fallen state and comfortability with darkness kept him more aware of the dark than the light. And as He came to His own, they rejected Him, but the sad truth is that right now, at this very moment, the light is still dismissed even in the church. If we deny the light, we deny the love. The reason men run from the light is fear of exposure. Men want to avoid the light to stay in the darkness because it brings instant gratification to those unholy desires and cravings. The light of Jesus enlightens us and brings us into the truth, and as truth is revealed and received, the light exposes residue and traces of sin. The more the light shines and exposes the troubled areas, the more we can adequately address those issues by confession, repentance, renouncing, and then turning in the direction of His will.

We must understand that when the Father takes the time to expose us when we are in sin, it's love in action! It is the loving heart of a good Father desiring the best for His children, even when we don't reciprocate that love. But humanity must turn back to its first love. The harder we purpose to love like Christ and sustain our faith, the mountains move because we showed up! The devil doesn't stand a chance against the unconditional love of Jesus Christ. He knows the authority, power, and weight that it carries more than some Christians. God is waiting for us to pull Heaven down into the Earth by the authority of Christ, our position, and our identity in love! We have access to Heaven and the keys to bind and loose, but why do we allow the light to dim on our watch?

We keep pretending we are okay, but the evidence proves otherwise! Why is it more important to address the people in the room of our life rather than submit to God? Why are we more taken with people knowing us rather than the Father knowing us? You see, religion cares nothing about relationships. It only seeks its desires. Consider how Jesus overturned the tables in the temple because the religious leaders were desecrating the very place designated for worship and prayer. If Jesus says it has to go, this should be the response of the church! If Jesus is disturbed by the lack of reverence for His Father's house, shouldn't we the more?

The thing in the church, with the assignment to shift us further away from the presence of God, is religion! It (this religion) will make room for everything else; mammon, idols, programs, bingo night, cliques, and coffee workshops, but will push out prayer, the part of the ministry that supports the whole church. No person ever got healed and delivered by religion. Jesus cautioned the disciples and the crowds of people standing by against ignoring the scriptures and following the righteousness of the religious leaders.

> *"So if you ignore the least commandment and teach others to do the same, you will be called the least in the Kingdom of Heaven. But anyone who obeys God's laws and teaches them will be called great in the Kingdom of Heaven. "But I warn you—unless your righteousness is better than the righteousness of the teachers of religious law and the Pharisees, you will never enter the*

Kingdom of Heaven!" **-Matthew 5:19-20 NLT**

"Jesus entered the Temple and began to drive out all the people buying and selling animals for sacrifice. He knocked over the tables of the money changers and the chairs of those selling doves. He said to them, "The Scriptures declare, 'My Temple will be called a house of prayer,' but you have turned it into a den of thieves!" **-Matthew 21:12-13 NLT**

Religion abhors relationships, but this spirit will go so far as to kill anyone in its way. It wants to kill the grace of God in your life! It wants to kill the truth and the love of God! You may say that's going a bit far, but the scriptures speak for themselves.

"The leading priests and teachers of religious law were plotting how to kill Jesus, but they were afraid of the people's reaction." **-Luke 22:2 NLT**

Will you look at how the spirit of religion works? It secretly gets angry and plots to kill anything that represents truth, love, grace, and worship, but its weakness is man's reaction. It is 100% concerned about the people's response. They (the religious leaders) were not afraid to kill the Son of God, but they were fearful of the people's reaction. Why is this? This spirit's primary goal is to operate like God, and the very thing it lives for is man's attention. It thrives off of man's attention, yet it seeks to enslave the same audience it craves!! And we wonder why it looks as if the church is following behind Jesus at a distance. It's because she is! If we take a sober look at the posture and attitude of the church, it appears as if she is a spectator rather than the radiant power God has graced her to be.

It's time to rise, Body of Christ, and be about the Father's business! It's time to rise, Ekklesia, for you are the called out, chosen, anointed bride walking in truth and love! You were created to worship. You are equipped with authority and power! Who told you, you were only a spectator at your wedding? Who told you, you could only pretend to be free? Rise out of despair and despondency. Lay your hands on the sick and watch them recover! Command scales to fall off of eyes, and they will see! Cast out demons and see the oppressed live free! You were built for this. But you must be the first partaker of the same grace that saved you, the very Truth that freed you, and the very Love that made the greatest investment! Yes, you must mount up on wings like eagles and soar in your purpose. It's time for you to shine and be radiant!! For then and only then can you advance the Kingdom of Heaven!

> *"Then he called his twelve disciples together and gave them power and authority over all devils, and power to cure diseases."* **-Luke 9:1 (KJV)**

> *"And when he had called unto him his twelve disciples, he gave them power against unclean spirits, to cast them out, and to heal all manner of sickness and all manner of disease."* **-Matthew 10:1 (KJV)**

> *"And my God will supply every need of yours according to his riches in glory in Christ Jesus."* **-Philippians 4:19 (ESV)**

> *"Even youths shall faint and be weary, and young men shall fall exhausted; but they who wait for the Lord shall renew their strength; they shall mount up with wings like eagles; they shall run and not be weary; they shall walk and not faint."* **-Isaiah 40:30-31 (ESV)**

So, if there is ever a time to know the Father intimately, it's right now! Sadly, it's the numbness and callousness of man's heart due to unbelief, religion, and disobedience to the Gospel of Jesus Christ that has prevented and even hindered the light from coming in the temple. Where there is no light, there is no love. I will not leave this statement to stand alone, but scripture always speaks for itself.

> *"For this people's heart has grown callous; their ears are hard of hearing,*

> *and they have shut their eyes; otherwise they might see with their eyes, and hear with their ears, and understand with their hearts, and turn back — and I would heal them."* **-Matthew 13:15 (CSB)**

Satan's objective is to superimpose his deceptions over the word of God in your life, that your purpose may be downplayed and sabotaged, thereby leaving your destiny unfulfilled. He uses his ground troops to interfere daily by sending pride, distractions, and offenses to the believer's heart. This enemy of ours comes to steal, kill, and destroy. He uses the same three baits: the lust of the eyes, the lust of the flesh, and the pride of life.

It's easy to fall prey to Satan and his tactics when we attempt to hide the real issues of our hearts. Sadly, a large portion of the church has mastered how to keep their hearts under lock and key, but the danger is when the silent issues of the heart begin to surface. These contaminants start to run a full-court press, and before you know it, you spend more time guarding the mess instead of the word of truth, aka love!

The church is straying farther and farther away from God's presence. Have we become the thing we said we wouldn't be? Are we walking around deceived about our status while the world is sober about the truth they see in us? We look more like the world than we would care to admit. Our eyes have made too many adjustments and put us out of alignment with the true character of the church! The bride wants to keep on her tattered gown, stained veil, frayed and worn pantyhose with her mix-match shoes. But this was her state before the cross.

While our Savior was on the cross, there was a great exchange. The beatings, bruises, cuts, blood clots, and disfigurement transformed the runaway bride's structure, appearance, and plight. It's time for the church to see herself as the bride of Christ. The true character of the bride of Christ is one of dominion, authority, truth, love, holiness, mercy, honor, and she is radiant. She is preparing to come forth in glory, not having spots or wrinkles.

No matter the state of the church right now, the Father will ensure His Son's bride is glorious. Hallelujah Lord!! It is why in the meantime, the wheat and the tares must grow together but only temporarily. You must know that you are the wheat and desire to be wheat! You must desire to be substantial if you plan on meeting the needs of others.

Jesus tells His disciples to eat His flesh and drink His blood because He understood His value to humankind. He understood the cup of suffering He would have to drink through the shedding of His blood and the breaking of His body. Jesus was the bread of Heaven that was come down into the world as the source of man's life. Because He is substance, the church has to be substance. The bride of Christ must always have a meaningful life that can supply a need to a dying world! So, I ask the question, "Are you substance?" Is your life progressively getting better, where people can thrive off of the Christ in you? You must keep your lights burning! It is the burning of your lamps that signifies your readiness for the bride- groom!

Take a moment and meditate on the scriptures below. Then, ask the Holy Spirit to open the eyes of your understanding to see the importance of your readiness.

> *"Husbands, love your wives, just as Christ loved the church and gave himself up for her to make her holy, cleansing her by the washing with water through the word, and to present her to himself as a radiant church, without stain or wrinkle or any other blemish, but holy and blameless."* **-Ephesians 5:25-27 (NIV)**

> *"This is a profound mystery— but I am talking about Christ and the*

church." **-Ephesians 5:32 (NIV)**

"Be dressed for service and keep your lamps burning, as though you were waiting for your master to return from the wedding feast. Then you will be ready to open the door and let him in the moment he arrives and knocks. The servants who are ready and waiting for his return will be rewarded. I tell you the truth, he himself will seat them, put on an apron, and serve them as they sit and eat! He may come in the middle of the night or just before dawn. But whenever he comes, he will reward the servants who are ready." **-Luke 12:35-38 (NLT)**

"Let us rejoice and be glad and give him glory! For the wedding of the Lamb has come, and his bride has made herself ready." **-Revelations 19:7 (NIV)**

"I am jealous for you with a godly jealousy. I promised you to one husband, to Christ, so that I might present you as a pure virgin to him." **-2 Corinthians 11:2 (NIV)**

Let's take a moment to pray.

Father, in the name of Jesus, I thank You for this moment in time, and I'm grateful for the power of Your word. I understand that there is nothing hidden from Your eyes, but everything is open and naked. You see every detail about my life, and you know the very issues of my heart. So, I ask in Jesus' name that You would reveal the stubborn places, reveal the secret places, and bring conviction to my heart for change's sake! Transform me for service and grace me to do what I can't do in my strength. I don't want to be the holdup, but I want to be the solution as the church! I want my light to shine for Your glory, and I long to be substance for those in need of truth. Father, put hunger and thirst for righteousness on the inside of me. Let me not be the church that compromises, let me not be the hypocritical church, and Lord, please don't let me be the church that's not ready! Expose the hidden places of my heart that I may renounce every unclean place so the enemy will no longer have legal access to this temple. This house belongs to You, Lord! This temple will be a place of prayer and worship for your glory. Lord, purge me with hyssop, clean and wash me so that I am whiter than snow! Please uncover and unveil spiritual truths so that I may grow in every area of my life. Light up my heart for love's sake and let every trace of darkness trouble me. In Jesus' name, I pray. Amen.

Now that you have prayed, begin to carve out time to sit in the Lord's presence. Take your Bible and Love Treatment journal with you. I also suggest you take some paper towels. When we are in the presence of the Lord, deliverance could happen at any time, and you want to be prepared!

Anytime God wants you free is a time of rejoicing!! Hallelujah! You don't want to leave anything to chance or an opening for the devil. Ask the Holy Spirit to reveal every issue of your heart and as He reveals these areas, write them down. Don't worry about how much He may show you. Remember, He wants you free for your purpose! After He reveals those dark places, verbally "repent and then renounce" those areas.

Repent for those heart issues with Godly sorrow and then command the unwelcome guest to leave and go into the abyss, never to return, in Jesus' name! When you exercise your dominion authority, those unclean personalities must go! You may feel uncomfortable. It's not you, but those unwanted guests that entered in through an opening. There may also be anger, sadness, and guilt, but you keep commanding those unclean personalities to go! Go as far as God will grace you in getting free!

When going through deliverance, it's essential to let the unclean spirit know your temple belongs to the Lord! You may find yourself belching, yawning, and coughing. There may be flatulence and even tears. Just tarry (humbly and patiently wait for Heaven to respond on your behalf) until you sense great liberty or until the Lord releases you. I believe God will grace us to operate in a deliverance session to a certain degree depending on the stubbornness of the spirit that's been oppressing the believer. But don't be dismayed. There are deliverance ministries, and hopefully, you are planted in one. Set an appointment with your Pastor for a deliverance session because you don't want to entertain demons when you are serious about being a light in the earth.

I'm so thankful for the many times God has graced me to go through self-deliverance, as well as having a Pastor that took me through a deliverance session. But listen, don't minimize the power of corporate deliverance. I'm so thankful for all the weapons and tools the Lord graced us with for the sake of getting free and staying free! The power of love not only covers a multitude of sins but love also drives everything out of the temple that's trespassing!!

Hallelujah, Lord God, for the victory of Your people! Just know the Lord is your light and your salvation! Whom shall you fear? Trust and believe your light will shine for the world, but more importantly for the Father to get His glory!

Chapter 4

Victory Over Your Enemy Requires More Heart Checks

"If you are going to live in victory, your loyalty must be 100% in truth and 100% in exposing the sick areas of the heart." - Chrissy D. Carter

It's easy to assume everything is good in your walk because you have been operating in a victory. The assumption is, I must be doing something right if God is giving me the victory over my enemies. Sadly, we prematurely arrive at this conclusion, thinking that just because God is showing kindness, I must be in right standing with Him. Simply because He is still favoring you by showing mercy doesn't mean there are no areas of concern. The truth of the matter is that God can show kindness to whoever He wills with no strings attached. But what if He allows us to take a loss? It doesn't mean His love has changed towards us.

On the contrary, it confirms the power of His love even more. It is why the eyes of our understanding must be opened to conclude; He loves me enough to help me realize there is no victory apart from Him. If that means I have to suffer a loss, be humiliated, or eat humble pie, He will permit it!

Let's look at Hebrews 12:6 NLT. It reads, *"For the LORD disciplines those he loves, and he punishes each one he accepts as his child."* Do you see how discipline and punishment are by-products of His love? It's because we belong to God that He has every right to correct, discipline, and punish without us questioning His love and His role as our Heavenly Father. Let's go further. The Hebrew writer gives us, as believers, a friendly reminder and a gentle warning.

> *"And you have forgotten the exhortation that addresses you as sons: "My son, do not take lightly the discipline of the Lord, and do not lose heart when He rebukes you."* **-Hebrews 12:5 (BSB)**

Somewhere along the way, we lost the memo, and the thing God instructed us not to do, we are doing even more. The conviction for the sinful ways we entertain is becoming less and less. We have become accustomed to overriding the gentle nudging of the Holy Spirit. Even as He responds with mercy in an attempt to give us time to get it right, we habitually frustrate His grace. Hear me, there is a danger in disregarding the issues of your heart, and there are consequences for downplaying God's patience with us. There is nothing hidden from Him. Just as He showers down goodness, He sends adversity to get our attention to lead us to an opportunity for true repentance.

> *"Do not both adversity and good come from the mouth of the Most High? Why should any mortal man complain in view of your sins. Let us examine and test our ways, and turn back to the LORD."* **-Lamentations 3:38-40 (BSB)**

> *"I do not frustrate the grace of God: for if righteousness come by the law, then Christ is dead in vain."* **-Galatians 2:21 (KJV)**

> *"For all that is secret will eventually be brought into the open, and everything that is concealed will be brought to light and made known to all."* **-Luke 8:17 (NLT)**

The Bible says, "He will reign on the just as well as the unjust," and guess what, that's His prerogative. We error when we believe having victory over a situation means everything is good. What about the silent convictions we often override? The areas the Lord is ready to deal with, but we keep ignoring and downplaying. God is trying to get your attention about those hidden places of the heart we don't see as a threat because He knows those issues will derail our purpose.

David knew about this place all too well as he was defeating his enemies left and right. He earned victory after victory, but somewhere along the way, his refusal to deal with his silent convictions caused him to suffer losses in his household, one after the other. Winning battles means nothing if you are not adequately suited and prepared for the war. It is our commitment as sons of God to secure great wins in our own homes. It is where we gain our credibility.

> *David captured 1,000 chariots, 7,000 charioteers, and 20,000 foot soldiers. He crippled all the chariot horses except enough for 100 chariots. When Arameans from Damascus arrived to help King Hadadezer, David killed 22,000 of them. Then he placed several army garrisons in Damascus, the Aramean capital, and the Arameans became David's subjects and paid him tribute money. So, the Lord made David victorious wherever he went.*
>
> *King David dedicated all these gifts to the Lord, as he did with the silver and gold from the other nations he had defeated—*
>
> *So David became even more famous when he returned from destroying 18,000 Edomites in the Valley of Salt. He placed army garrisons throughout Edom, and all the Edomites became David's subjects. In fact, the Lord made David victorious wherever he went. So David reigned over all Israel and did what was just and right for all his people.* **-2 Samuel 8:4-6, 11, 13-15 (NLT)**

Do we believe that just because God is still giving us victories in areas of our life that it means our sin is hidden or put out of His sight? I would like to believe that because He is still showing mercy and kindness by granting us a victory, one we don't deserve, it's meant to win our love over for Him. We have been reckless with handling the Father's love towards us because we refuse to acknowledge the dark spots in our souls. We attempt to keep the provocative images, hidden lust, addictions, inward jealousy, etc., under lock and key. Yet, we keep nursing the unhealthy appetites, dress up, and show up for Sunday service. The longer you turn a deaf ear to the warnings, convictions, and even the love that shows up in the form of mercy, you are positioning yourself like David. David was near and dear to God's heart, but that didn't stop Him from giving David over to his lust problem so that he could experience restoration.

That's a nugget. God will give you over to your little god for the sake of your restoration. That is love in action!

We must be deliberate in checking our heart's condition because if you abandon a heart issue, you will inevitably enter a state of numbness. When you deliberately overlook the Holy Spirit's convictions and turn a deaf ear to the Word of God, your conscience is seared. You become a Christian who is numb to the things that grieve the Holy Spirit.

> *"To the pure, all things are pure; but to the defiled and unbelieving, nothing is pure. Indeed, both their minds and their consciences are defiled. They profess to know God, but by their actions they deny Him. They are detestable, disobedient and unfit for any good deed."* **-Titus 1:15-16 (BSB)**

"[misled] by the hypocrisy of liars whose consciences are seared as with a branding iron [leaving them incapable of ethical functioning]." **-1Timothy 4:2 (AMP)**

It's imperative to ask Jesus to shine His light on every area that's contrary to the will of the Father. It is crucial when He is growing you in your ministry, business, and personal relationships so He can get glory from these areas. Don't allow the victories against your enemies to decrease the momentum of your communion with the Lord. Instead, do the exact opposite and press in harder.

When we soberly review this chapter in 2 Samuel 8, David won, and God made him successful. If we were to liken David's victories to a 21st-century ministry, it would be thriving like crazy! Let me put more color to this parallel. Today, David's ministry would be a super strong mega ministry founded on prayer, intercession, and spiritual warfare, birthed from communion and intimacy. It would be his basic training as a shepherd boy, reliance on the Almighty God for the passion for serving in this capacity, and up-close tender moments with the sheep he tended. All of those things would open his heart to a love that required so much from him.

Even when considering that his earthly father had no idea of his true identity as king, God was tucking away this truth for an appointed time. Thus, we see this picture-perfect opportunity for God to open David's heart to birth patience, strength, focus on something other than himself, warfare tactics, and nurturing. It was a space and time for his gifts, call, and anointing to spring forth. God used the very thing his brothers looked down on to ready him. God used a season of being rejected by man as a training ground that solidified how favored he was by God! David's father and brothers considering him unfit to be a king show how man's rejection and undervalue of your purpose can separate you for serious training. Or to whip you in shape for the naysayers, haters, onlookers, spectators, and Goliaths in your life. It's an important nugget that you must grab. It's not always the people rejecting you; it's that God selected you and pulled you onto a different training ground.

Whatever lie the devil has spoken about your identity, please know the answer is always on the other side of what he has said. So, when you hear voices coming at you saying, "You're not loved!" It is your cue to confess I am loved! When he tells you that you won't be anything, and you will always be out here shoveling dung for these sheep, say, "I'm more than a conqueror, and I can do all things through Christ who strengthens me. I am the head and not the tail, above and not beneath!" And when you focus on where the Father has planted you, and you're determined to serve as unto the Lord, the prophet Samuel will be arriving soon to anoint you the king. Hold on and stay the course because something great is going to come out of this place! Hallelujah, Lord Jesus! We bless Your holy name for this place of grace! So, when we look at David's life before he walks into a dark season of sin, he was very successful. If he lived in this day and time, his ministry would significantly impact the land!

His ministry would meet the people's needs because of the strong leaders properly trained, positioned, and ready. David's ministry would be reaching and touching so many people because of his integrity and character. He demonstrates how to properly serve and reverence up-level leadership by showcasing his submission towards Saul, the one that was jealous of him and wanted to kill him. David models the way by not allowing anyone to harm Saul even while this unclean spirit of jealousy was harassing him. David also demonstrates the wisdom and power that comes when God answers you every time, so his ministry would prove to have a pretty good foundation.

As the ministry grows, the people are delivered and set free. God gives David success against his enemies, but he would be sustained by being naked and unashamed of the dark spots and dealing with those nasty, ugly spots! Sadly, this is what is happening right now with the church. God has been so good to His under-shepherds and increased the works of their hands. Still, the refusal to deal with the one dark spot and turning a deaf ear to the Holy Spirit's secret convictions has led them off the battlefield during the time kings go off to battle. The enemy has breached the server of spiritual convictions and left the holiest place in their walk to revisit the outer court. There is a danger when something in you causes you to change courts and pulls you out of the will of God. But wait, why is God allowing David to stay at home while his men are on the battlefield? God let David see what's in his heart and how far it will take him out of His divine will for proving purposes.

This should shed light on our situations, our walk, especially when we know the Holy Spirit has been convicting us of things that are not right and go against the will of God. We must quickly grab hold of this: whatever you refuse to expose will eventually expose you! Whatever the church continues to keep under wraps will inevitably become the stronghold that imprisons her! It would be better if we come clean with God so He can completely deliver us. Still, the deception positions us to lie to the one that hand-selected us from tending the sheep in the background to being crowned as king. God's love and goodness towards us has a way of revealing our level of character and maturity towards Him and for the assignment. One thing you must never forget is that there is nothing you can confess to your Father that will cause Him to stop loving you! It's time to come out of hiding because the longer you stay, the greater the sin becomes, the greater the consequences, and the harder the fall.

David experienced restoration because, after the adultery, the murder, and deception, the truth had to confront what was perverting and imprisoning God's vessel (set man). The very thing David refused to expose inside of him had now ravished and brought destruction and death to his house. But the moment David realized the prophet Nathan was confronting him with truth, he was so hurt, and Godly sorrow penetrated his heart. He realized that he had sinned against God. It was then he penned Psalm 51.

"Have mercy on me, O God, because of your unfailing love. Because of your great compassion, blot out the stain of my sins. Wash me clean from my guilt.

Purify me from my sin. For I recognize my rebellion; it haunts me day and night. Against you, and you alone, have I sinned; I have done what is evil in your sight. You will be proved right in what you say, and your judgment against me is just.

For I was born a sinner— yes, from the moment my mother conceived me. But you desire honesty from the womb, teaching me wisdom even there. Purify me from my sins, and I will be clean; wash me, and I will be whiter than snow. Oh, give me back my joy again; you have broken me— now let me rejoice. Don't keep looking at my sins. Remove the stain of my guilt. Create in me a clean heart, O God. Renew a loyal spirit within me. Do not banish me from your presence, and don't take your Holy Spirit from me. Restore to me the joy of your salvation, and make me willing to obey you. Then I will teach your ways to rebels, and

they will return to you. Forgive me for shedding blood, O God who saves; then I will joyfully sing of your forgiveness. Unseal my lips, O Lord, that my mouth may praise you. You do not desire a sacrifice, or I would offer one.

You do not want a burnt offering. The sacrifice you desire is a broken spirit.

> *You will not reject a broken and repentant heart, O God."* -**Psalms 51:1-17 (NLT)**

When we look at David's response to being exposed for sinning against God, he didn't just throw some words together and say I'm sorry. Instead, he went to God with a broken spirit, a broken and a contrite heart. He was torn up on the inside because he hurt God and not because he got caught. It wasn't because he was trying to keep his followers, and it wasn't because he didn't want to lose his position with man or his wealth. No, this was a moment where David bypassed his soul, and his spirit had an encounter with his Father. He said, please don't take your Holy Spirit from me but restore to me the joy of Your salvation. Father, help me obey You so I can teach the rebels Your ways, and they will turn back to you! Let this Psalm become the standard of repentance that opens you up to a level of love you have never known. David was overwhelmed by God's mercy and forgiveness. He knew he didn't deserve it because he sinned against God and failed the sheep he was expected to protect. It was a weight and burden that was greater than Goliath, the lion, and the bear. This level of repentance broke the barrier of sin and guilt separating David from his Heavenly Father.

> *"But David persisted. "I have been taking care of my father's sheep and goats," he said. "When a lion or a bear comes to steal a lamb from the flock, I go after it with a club and rescue the lamb from its mouth. If the animal turns on me, I catch it by the jaw and club it to death. I have done this to both lions and bears, and I'll do it to this pagan Philistine, too, for he has defied the armies of the living God!"* **-1 Samuel 17:34-36 (NLT)**

David experienced a love that swept him off his feet. He was entangled with the lion of the tribe of Judah, the Lord of his salvation. The Lord flooded his heart with doses of Agape Treatments! It was this defining moment in David's life that would forever transform him.

If there is a heavy weight of guilt resting on you, you are trapped and don't know how to break free; the key is willingly exposing what's oppressing and imprisoning you! Then, when you confess it to God, and there is Godly sorrow, you will surely experience freedom! Ask the Holy Spirit to lead and guide you into all truth and make a sober decision to let the unconditional love of Christ win in you.

Chapter 5

The Power of Silent Love

"Just because you can't trace the feeling of Love doesn't mean He is not actively at work in your life." - Chrissy Carter

When love is silent, don't discount its ability to complete the mission. It's on assignment to conquer the darkness and enemies of hell you can't fight off on your own. So, in the silence, there is a shifting that positions you for victory!! Love was conquering death, hell, and the grave when it seemed as if there was no activity, but the silence is not the absence of movement. The silence is not the absence of breakthrough! The silence is not the absence of empowerment and strength!

Hallelujah to the Lamb of God who takes away all sins of the world! In silence, the kingdom of darkness was overtaken and enslaved and given boundaries to operate. While the disciples thought ministry had stopped and the religious leaders thought their wicked plan to kill Jesus was a success, love was on a "secret service assignment!" He was taking keys from death, hell, and the grave! It was an underground, unseen, hostile takeover that would forever change and permanently transform all of humanity! There is power in silent love, especially when it appears nothing is happening. God will take a moment of silence and turn everything wrong in your life around for your good! When Jesus was being persecuted and questioned, He didn't utter a word. When the woman was caught in adultery and her accusers were ready to stone her, Jesus quietly stooped down to write on the pavement of the temple.

Oh, but wait, where was the man who had a wife already but was laying with this woman? Why was the spirit of religion so eager to kill this woman but silent about her crime partner? Sadly, there is another silent power in the scriptures at work in this text called silent deception. We must realize, just because the enemy has clipped out a portion of your life's story to use against you and bring charges against you, doesn't mean it's going to prevail! The truth will prevail in your situation when you trust. Even when you don't see immediate justice, you must have a holy resolve to wait on the mighty hand of love.

According to the law, both parties found in adultery are stoned to death. But the Pharisees, the religious leaders of the law, did not know nor understand the power behind this silent love! So why was Jesus writing and not talking at this moment? Simply put, He was teaching. School was in session for this woman and her accusers, and there was silence during a test.

> *"If a man commits adultery with his neighbor's wife, both the man and the woman who have committed adultery must be put to death."* **-Leviticus 20:10 (NLT)**

So, where is the other guilty party in this text? Where is the man, and why do they willingly omit his part in this act? We see it's not because they were upright leaders of the truth and were certainly not operating in love. They conspired, but silent love was in motion, in operation, and was covering! That's what love does, it covers a multitude of sins, and it always teams up with truth to bring about justice. Stop worrying and trust the never-ending power of His love for your situation. You won't add anything but longer delays without faith. Now, let's go further in this text.

Jesus already knew the accusers' motives. In this moment of silence, the objective was to remind them that His Father's law was greater than their opinions, criticism, and finger-pointing at this woman. It could in no way overpower the Word of God. The Bible says Jesus stooped down. I believe this lowly position and posture was significant because this was a message of the power of humility that the Pharisees and Scribes lacked and needed to imitate. In this low position, Jesus sent so many messages to the woman, the accusers, and us. I believe He could identify with the woman's humiliation because He knew those same stones would be thrown at Him.

Jesus says, "He who is without sin, cast the first stone," and one by one, her accusers left. I believe that whatever words He wrote in silence had great power manifested in such a way that the atmosphere shifted. They sealed the enemy's mouth and caused every one of the woman's accusers to walk away. In my Holy Ghost imagination, I see Jesus writing the names of everyone that had a stone in their hand, along with their deliberate, sinful acts.

> *"Jesus straightened up and asked her, "Woman, where are they? Has no one condemned you?" "No one Sir," she replied. "Then neither do I condemn you," Jesus declared. "Go now and leave your life of sin."* **-John 8:10-11 (NIV)**

We see that Jesus (Love) didn't condemn the woman, but He ensured she understood that He in no way ignored or condoned her life of sin. Her turning point was when she wholeheartedly turned away from the sin, a heart transplant that would set her up for a clean living and a new life in Jesus Christ.

Listen, stop trying to figure out the moves; just let love lead the way and yield. Picture yourself dancing with love, and you don't know the moves. Well, your objective is to be in sync with the moves, and that's going to happen when you live a John 15 lifestyle. Live in the vine, reside in the vine, stay connected because it's your connection that causes you to sense a move change. The more you know Him, know His ways, character, and likes and dislikes, the more you will feel His love.

You must know the Word intimately to flow with Him, even when you can't trace Him. I had my moments of silence with God, where He revealed to me that I had to step back and rely on Him to work. The intention was to pull up my faith. Still, for a moment, the Holy Spirit revealed I was flinching during a season I was supposed to be trusting Him for a breakthrough in my son's life. When He pointed it out and walked me through to a place called rest, it was a sweet, quiet time for me as I watched some troublesome situations right before my eyes.

Of course, I was still interceding, fasting, and trusting God. This was when He ministered to me about silent love, and now He was gracing me to walk through it. Did I have some days where I missed it? Absolutely, but the Holy Spirit helped me get right back into position and in a prayerful posture. There were many fires going all at once during this season in my life, but God was doing something in me to pull my faith up to trust mode! I'm still in trust mode, but it isn't always easy. Still, there is grace to overcome the enemy's fires that come for your family, your seed, and your marriage. Those are times where God will use you as a weapon of mass destruction against the kingdom of darkness without physically putting your hands on the situation. If we are not careful, the hands-on approach can keep the fires spreading because now we are distracted and too close to the danger. The view is obscured when we are too close, but when the Lord pulls you up and your seating changes, you are seated with Christ Jesus in heavenly places; it's an automatic win!

You fight better from this place; you see better and further. The problem gets so tiny you can't see it! Hallelujah, Lord Jesus! All the while, things are swiftly moving into place! Finally, you realize no one loves your spouse, children, children in the faith that you under-shepherd or your family as much as our Heavenly Father! He already proved it when He sent His only begotten son to die for us on that cross! What a love!

Chapter 6

All Talk and No Action Type of Love

"Dear children, let's not merely say that we love each other; let us show the truth by our actions." **-1 John 3:18 (NLT)**

How often have you been in the company of people who always knew the right things to say, conveyed knowledge on the right level for their audience, and shared wisdom that could cause a house to change and thrive? But they are living the opposite of what they put out. My husband knew a person like this, and for privacy's sake, we will call him Sir.

Sir had access to the words of life and knew how to coach others into doing the right thing for their situation, but he would not apply it to his life. My thoughts are, how can you be okay with counseling a couple that has a strained marriage? The couple is wise enough to seek a lifeline from the word of truth. Still, the man or woman of God they're seeking counseling from is not living the quality of life that brings glory and honor to God. They are deliberately living the opposite of what they are counseling others on. That is what Sir was doing.

When you take the time to process this picture, you can see the hypocrisy and deception, but how often does our life's story take on this same hypocritical stance? In reality, we see a double standard living too often in the church. But no one wants to confront or deal with it, only slapping band-aids on areas that need spiritual heart surgery.

When this quality of living defines our roles as Christians, there is only one area that we must issue an audit: our love. Jesus said, "If you love Me, keep My commandments." The fact that we compromise and pick and choose what portion of the word we want to live reveals we have been weighed on the scales and found wanting (at a deficient). If Jesus told us that keeping some of His commandments would prove we love Him, maybe our standard would be justified, but He understood the power of love in action! Are we representing Christ's love fully and completely, or do we think more highly of ourselves than we ought? Unfortunately, we don't impact people's lives to the point of change because they see the real us. They hear what we say, and please rest assure, they watch what we do! The mouth can boast great things, but if the intimate details of your life don't line up, credibility is out the window. Simply put, actions speak louder than words!

> *"But don't just listen to God's word. You must do what it says. Otherwise, you are only fooling yourself."* **-James 1:22 (NLT)**

James stated in verse 21, "*Therefore get rid of all moral filth and every expression of evil and humbly accept the word planted in you, which can save your soul.*" When we see the word, therefore, we know James is dealing with an area in the church that must be addressed. When we read verses 19-20, he is pulling the covers back on the selfishness of man when his focus is on what he has to say rather than what he needs to hear. So, he instructs them to be quick to hear, slow to speak, and slow to get angry. Why? Because human anger does not produce the righteousness of God because its only agenda is to promote self. Therefore or (for that reason), we must get rid of all moral filth. This moral filth deals with impure living, all the stuff that's wrong in our life that does not line up with the will of God. James says, "humbly accept or receive with meekness the implanted word of God." This is the only way to receive, in humility, that our soul may be saved to the uttermost.

We have attempted to make edits and changes to the Word of God to fit our life. This is why God's love isn't felt, seen, and demonstrated in such a way that glorifies God and impacts lives. The truth is our efforts have set us back because we are not ridding ourselves of the filth but we still sit under the word of truth, thinking we are okay. Sadly, there is no way for truth to take root because we are weighed down with the issues of life, the cares of this world, the last bad breakup, the pain of the abuse, the failed marriage, the loss of a loved one, and so much more. These are the things that create hard places/spots in the heart that spills over into our actions. Yet we are trying to move forward and see a scenery change take place in our story. Instead, it seems like nothing is changing, and we keep finding ourselves here! Right here in this place, that's taking life from us. We are screaming on the inside while smiling and being there for our spouse and best friend. We're on the job attempting to put our best foot forward, but the question is, who are you fooling? It's time to undress the real issues of the heart so we can operate like the real church.

It is our reasonable service as the church to have the mindset that love will not fail me! I will fail, jobs will fail, people will fail me, but love will always manifest His presence in our situation! We are called to keep the doors of the church open at all times. You may ask, "How is that possible?" It's possible because you are the church. Jesus said to them in Luke 19:46 NLT, *"The Scriptures declare, 'My Temple will be a house of prayer,' but you have turned it into a den of thieves."*

You must understand that we are the Church, and that agape love is supposed to live inside while impacting the outside. We can no longer be okay with just talking about this love or singing about Him. Yes, love is He, Jesus Christ, our Savior! WE MUST LIVE LOVE! As you receive your daily doses from Him, be deliberate and inject someone else with the Love that's inside of you! I decree that the love of Christ in you shall change and transform environments, situations, people, mindsets, responses, cities, and nations. But more importantly, this love is moment by moment transforming you into a "Love Agent" in the earth, in Jesus' Name! Amen!

Daily Doses of Love Scriptures

Use these scriptures as your time of devotion and prayer concerning any areas in this chapter you know you need healing and deliverance. If I were you, nothing would be left to chance. This is your book to highlight, underline, or circle those key things the Lord is ministering to you about. Meditate on a scripture a day. When you meditate, you plan in your mind how to walk out the Word of God. Expect these love doses to shift you from conditional love to unconditional love! Hallelujah, Lord Jesus!

"The one who does not love has not become acquainted with God [does not and never did know Him], for God is love. [He is the originator of love, and it is an enduring attribute of His nature.]" -1 John 4:8 (AMP)

"Dear friends, let us continue to love one another, for love comes from God. Anyone who loves is a child of God and knows God." -1 John 4:7 (NLT)

"God showed how much he loved us by sending his one and only Son into the world so that we might have eternal life through him. This is real love— not that we loved God, but that he loved us and sent his Son as a sacrifice to take away our sins." -1 John 4:9-10 NLT

"Dear friends, since God loved us that much, we surely ought to love each other. No one has ever seen God. But if we love each other, God lives in us, and his love is brought to full expression in us. And God has given us his Spirit as proof that we live in him and he in us.

All who declare that Jesus is the Son of God have God living in them, and they live in God. We know how much God loves us, and we have put our trust in his love. God is love, and all who live in love live in God, and God lives in them." -1 John 4:11-13, 15-16 (NLT)

"And as we live in God, our love grows more perfect. So we will not be afraid on the day of judgment, but we can face him with confidence because we live like Jesus here in this world. Such love has no fear, because perfect love expels all fear. If we are afraid, it is for fear of punishment, and this shows that we have not fully experienced his perfect love. We love each other because he loved us first." -1 John 4:17-19 (NLT)

"If someone says, "I love God," but hates a fellow believer, that person is a liar; for if we don't love people we can see, how can we love God, whom we cannot see? And he has given us this command: Those who love God must also love their fellow believers." -1 John 4:20-21 (NLT)

Daily Doses of Love Scriptures

Use these scriptures as your time of devotion and prayer concerning any areas in this chapter you know you need healing and deliverance. If I were you, nothing would be left to chance. This is your book to highlight, underline, or circle those key things the Lord is ministering to you about. Meditate on a scripture a day. When you meditate, you plan in your mind how to walk out the Word of God. Expect these love doses to shift you from conditional love to unconditional love! Hallelujah, Lord Jesus!

"Everyone who believes that Jesus is the Christ has become a child of God. And everyone who loves the Father loves his children, too. We know we love God's children if we love God and obey his commandments. Loving God means keeping his commandments, and his commandments are not burdensome." -1 John 5:1-3 (NLT)

"We know that God's children do not make a practice of sinning, for God's Son holds them securely, and the evil one cannot touch them.

Dear children, keep away from anything that might take God's place in your hearts." -1 John 5:18, 21 (NLT)

"For this is how God loved the world: He gave his one and only Son, so that everyone who believes in him will not perish but have eternal life."- John 3:16 NLT

"But God showed his great love for us by sending Christ to die for us while we were still sinners. And since we have been made right in God's sight by the blood of Christ, he will certainly save us from God's condemnation. For since our friendship with God was restored by the death of his Son while we were still his enemies, we will certainly be saved through the life of his Son. So now we can rejoice in our wonderful new relationship with God because our Lord Jesus Christ has made us friends of God." -Romans 5:8-11 (NLT)

"But to you who are willing to listen, I say, love your enemies! Do good to those who hate you. Bless those who curse you. Pray for those who hurt you.

If someone slaps you on one cheek, offer the other cheek also. If someone demands your coat, offer your shirt also. Give to anyone who asks; and when things are taken away from you, don't try to get them back. Do to others as you would like them to do to you. "If you love only those who love you, why should you get credit for that? Even sinners love those who love them! And if you do good only to those who do good to you, why should you get credit?

Even sinners do that much! And if you lend money only to those who can repay you, why should you get credit? Even sinners will lend to other sinners for a full return. "Love your enemies! Do good to them. Lend to them without expecting to be repaid. Then your reward from heaven will be very great, and you will truly be acting as children of the Most High, for he is kind to those who are unthankful and wicked. You must be compassionate, just as your Father is compassionate." -Luke 6:27-36 (NLT)

Daily Doses of Love Scriptures

Use these scriptures as your time of devotion and prayer concerning any areas in this chapter you know you need healing and deliverance. If I were you, nothing would be left to chance. This is your book to highlight, underline, or circle those key things the Lord is ministering to you about. Meditate on a scripture a day. When you meditate, you plan in your mind how to walk out the Word of God. Expect these love doses to shift you from conditional love to unconditional love! Hallelujah, Lord Jesus!

"And I am convinced that nothing can ever separate us from God's love. Neither death nor life, neither angels nor demons, neither our fears for today nor our worries about tomorrow—not even the powers of hell can separate us from God's love." -Romans 8:38 (NLT)

"This is the message you have heard from the beginning: We should love one another. We must not be like Cain, who belonged to the evil one and killed his brother. And why did he kill him? Because Cain had been doing what was evil, and his brother had been doing what was righteous.

If we love our brothers and sisters who are believers, it proves that we have passed from death to life. But a person who has no love is still dead. Anyone who hates another brother or sister is really a murderer at heart. And you know that murderers don't have eternal life within them." -1 John 3:11-12, 14-15 (NLT)

"We know what real love is because Jesus gave up his life for us. So we also ought to give up our lives for our brothers and sisters. If someone has enough money to live well and sees a brother or sister in need but shows no compassion—how can God's love be in that person? Dear children, let's not merely say that we love each other; let us show the truth by our actions. Our actions will show that we belong to the truth, so we will be confident when we stand before God.

And this is his commandment: We must believe in the name of his Son, Jesus Christ, and love one another, just as he commanded us." -1 John 3:16-19, 23 (NLT)

"Most important of all, continue to show deep love for each other, for love covers a multitude of sins." -1 Peter 4:8 (NLT)

Daily Doses of Love Scriptures

Use these scriptures as your time of devotion and prayer concerning any areas in this chapter you know you need healing and deliverance. If I were you, nothing would be left to chance. This is your book to highlight, underline, or circle those key things the Lord is ministering to you about. Meditate on a scripture a day. When you meditate, you plan in your mind how to walk out the Word of God. Expect these love doses to shift you from conditional love to unconditional love! Hallelujah, Lord Jesus!

"And may you have the power to understand, as all God's people should, how wide, how long, how high, and how deep his love is. May you experience the love of Christ, though it is too great to understand fully. Then you will be made complete with all the fullness of life and power that comes from God." -Ephesians 3:18-19 (NLT)

"When I think of all this, I fall to my knees and pray to the Father, the Creator of everything in heaven and on earth. I pray that from his glorious, unlimited resources he will empower you with inner strength through his Spirit. Then Christ will make his home in your hearts as you trust in him. Your roots will grow down into God's love and keep you strong." -Ephesians 3:14-17 (NLT)

"Your love for one another will prove to the world that you are my disciples." -John 13:35 (NLT)

"Jesus replied, "'You must love the LORD your God with all your heart, all your soul, and all your mind.' This is the first and greatest commandment. A second is equally important: 'Love your neighbor as yourself.'" -Matthew 22:37-39 (NLT)

"Love each other with genuine affection and take delight in honoring each other." -Romans 12:10 (NLT)

"Don't just pretend to love others. Really love them. Hate what is wrong. Hold tightly to what is good." -Romans 12:9 (NLT)

"Since God chose you to be the holy people he loves, you must clothe yourselves with tenderhearted mercy, kindness, humility, gentleness, and patience. Make allowance for each other's faults, and forgive anyone who offends you. Remember, the Lord forgave you, so you must forgive others. Above all, clothe yourselves with love, which binds us all together in perfect harmony. And let the peace that comes from Christ rule in your hearts. For as members of one body you are called to live in peace. And always be thankful." -Colossians 3:12-15 (NLT)

Daily Doses of Love Scriptures

Use these scriptures as your time of devotion and prayer concerning any areas in this chapter you know you need healing and deliverance. If I were you, nothing would be left to chance. This is your book to highlight, underline, or circle those key things the Lord is ministering to you about. Meditate on a scripture a day. When you meditate, you plan in your mind how to walk out the Word of God. Expect these love doses to shift you from conditional love to unconditional love! Hallelujah, Lord Jesus!

"Wives, submit to your husbands, as is fitting for those who belong to the Lord. Husbands, love your wives and never treat them harshly. Children, always obey your parents, for this pleases the Lord. Fathers, do not aggravate your children, or they will become discouraged. Slaves, obey your earthly masters in everything you do. Try to please them all the time, not just when they are watching you. Serve them sincerely because of your reverent fear of the Lord. Work willingly at whatever you do, as though you were working for the Lord rather than for people. Remember that the Lord will give you an inheritance as your reward, and that the Master you are serving is Christ. But if you do what is wrong, you will be paid back for the wrong you have done. For God has no favorites." -Colossians 3:18-25 (NLT)

"But the Holy Spirit produces this kind of fruit in our lives: love, joy, peace, patience, kindness, goodness, faithfulness, gentleness, and self-control. There is no law against these things! Those who belong to Christ Jesus have nailed the passions and desires of their sinful nature to his cross and crucified them there. Since we are living by the Spirit, let us follow the Spirit's leading in every part of our lives." -Galatians 5:22-25 (NLT)

"Therefore I, a prisoner for serving the Lord, beg you to lead a life worthy of your calling, for you have been called by God. Always be humble and gentle. Be patient with each other, making allowance for each other's faults because of your love. Make every effort to keep yourselves united in the Spirit, binding yourselves together with peace.

Then we will no longer be immature like children. We won't be tossed and blown about by every wind of new teaching. We will not be influenced when people try to trick us with lies so clever they sound like the truth. Instead, we will speak the truth in love, growing in every way more and more like Christ, who is the head of his body, the church." -Ephesians 4:1-3, 14-15 (NLT)

"And do not bring sorrow to God's Holy Spirit by the way you live. Remember, he has identified you as his own, guaranteeing that you will be saved on the day of redemption. Get rid of all bitterness, rage, anger, harsh words, and slander, as well as all types of evil behavior. Instead, be kind to each other, tenderhearted, forgiving one another, just as God through Christ has forgiven you." -Ephesians 4:30-32 (NLT)

"Don't look out only for your own interests, but take an interest in others, too." -Philippians 2:4 (NLT)

"Therefore if there is any encouragement and comfort in Christ [as there certainly is in abundance], if there is any consolation of love, if there is any fellowship [that we share] in the Spirit, if [there is] any [great depth of] affection and compassion, make my joy complete by being of the same mind, having the same love [toward one another], knit together in spirit, intent on one purpose [and living a life that reflects your faith and spreads the gospel— the good news regarding salvation through faith in Christ]." -Philippians 2:1-2 (AMP)

Daily Doses of Love Scriptures

Use these scriptures as your time of devotion and prayer concerning any areas in this chapter you know you need healing and deliverance. If I were you, nothing would be left to chance. This is your book to highlight, underline, or circle those key things the Lord is ministering to you about. Meditate on a scripture a day. When you meditate, you plan in your mind how to walk out the Word of God. Expect these love doses to shift you from conditional love to unconditional love! Hallelujah, Lord Jesus!

"Do nothing from selfishness or empty conceit [through factional motives, or strife], but with [an attitude of] humility [being neither arrogant nor self- righteous], regard others as more important than yourselves.

Have this same attitude in yourselves which was in Christ Jesus [look to Him as your example in selfless humility]," -Philippians 2:3, 5 (AMP)

"Don't just pretend to love others. Really love them. Hate what is wrong. Hold tightly to what is good. Love each other with genuine affection, and take delight in honoring each other.

Rejoice in our confident hope. Be patient in trouble, and keep on praying. When God's people are in need, be ready to help them. Always be eager to practice hospitality. Bless those who persecute you. Don't curse them; pray that God will bless them. Be happy with those who are happy, and weep with those who weep. Live in harmony with each other. Don't be too proud to enjoy the company of ordinary people. And don't think you know it all! Never pay back evil with more evil. Do things in such a way that everyone can see you are honorable. Do all that you can to live in peace with everyone." -Romans 12:9-10, 12-18 (NLT)

"All praise to God, the Father of our Lord Jesus Christ, who has blessed us with every spiritual blessing in the heavenly realms because we are united with Christ. Even before he made the world, God loved us and chose us in Christ to be holy and without fault in his eyes.

So we praise God for the glorious grace he has poured out on us who belong to his dear Son. He is so rich in kindness and grace that he purchased our freedom with the blood of his Son and forgave our sins. He has showered his kindness on us, along with all wisdom and understanding." -Ephesians 1:3-4, 6-8 (NLT)

"If I could speak all the languages of earth and of angels, but didn't love others, I would only be a noisy gong or a clanging cymbal. If I had the gift of prophecy, and if I understood all of God's secret plans and possessed all knowledge, and if I had such faith that I could move mountains, but didn't love others, I would be nothing. If I gave everything I have to the poor and even sacrificed my body, I could boast about it; but if I didn't love others, I would have gained nothing. Love is patient and kind. Love is not jealous or boastful or proud or rude. It does not demand its own way. It is not irritable, and it keeps no record of being wronged. It does not rejoice about injustice but rejoices whenever the truth wins out. Love never gives up, never loses faith, is always hopeful, and endures through every circumstance." -1 Corinthians 13:1-7 (NLT)

Matters of the Heart

This area of the book allows you to do some personal journaling, and you have the opportunity to use it as a daily spiritual "EKG Reading." Take this time to assess how this Word applies to your life and address your heart's issues at this present moment.

Date/Time: ________

Symptoms: (ex. I'm normally on edge, stressed, holding on to things or I get offended easily). Please be very honest with where you are. Ask the Holy Spirit to reveal what you can't see.

____

____

____

How does the truth about where you are in your love walk make you feel?

____

____

____

Do you feel like this book would be perfect for....? (someone else) Do you feel justified, condemned, or convicted? It's important to pinpoint this area because that determines how you respond to these love treatments. There is absolutely nothing wrong with wanting others to be blessed, but when you read or hear spiritual truths meant to make you free and your focus is on how someone else needs this truth, there are areas of denial and possibly a blind spot. If you recognize you have some spiritual diseases or disorders but refuse to deal with them, you have to ask, is this pride, shame, avoidance that stems from the fear of knowing the truth? The level of honesty determines your level of breakthrough.

____

____

____

____

____

____

____

____

____

Diseases, Disorders, and Plagues that Cause Spiritual Heart Trouble

Envy
Abuse
Accusations
Afflictions
Immorality
Jealousy
Fear
Abandonment
Anxiety
Contempt
Pride
Condemnation
Rejection
Rebellion
Stubbornness
Selfishness
Worry
Witchcraft
Soul-Ties
Cursing
Gluttony
Pain
Grief

Offenses
Anger
Argumentative
Bitterness
Blindspots
Complaining
Complacency
Covetousness
Deception
Depression
Divorce
Disobedience
Insecurity
Finger Pointing
Fault-Finding
Division
Strife
Arguments
Loneliness
Isolation
Poverty
Debt
Religion

Revenge
Doubt
Frustration
Generational
Curses
Gossip
Unforgiveness
Irritation
Corruption
Habits
Adultery
Fornication
Competition
Denial
Racism
Manipulation
Lust (eyes, flesh)
Mean-spirited
Carnal
Slander
Compromise
Idolatry
Hardships

Addiction (alcohol, drugs, cigarettes, gambling, food, and porn)
Love of mammon/money
Hate, Spite, and More
Suicidal tendencies

Notes for Your 7 Day Love Treatments

Day 1:

Day 2:

Day 3:

Day 4:

Day 5:

____

____

____

____

Day 6:

____

____

____

____

Day 7:

____

____

____

____

Closure Words

We, the church, must heed Matthew 24:12, "Because of the increase of wickedness, the love of most will grow cold." If there was ever a time we needed healing in the land, it's right now. Jesus was preparing the disciples for harsh conditions within their society. But this scripture also forecasts what is coming in the world we live in.

Sadly, the heart that grows cold is more dangerous than persecution on the outside of the church. Why? Because cold love is an inside job, it does more damage inside the church than the persecution coming from the outside. This is why we must guard our hearts with all diligence, for out of it comes the issues of life. (Proverbs 4:23) We also must be sure we are the solution and not the problem. The body of Christ is called to love on a level that's always covering others in their shortcomings, but we must first address the issues of our hearts.

If God gets glory out of us, we must love the Lord our God with all our heart, mind, soul, and strength. We must love our neighbors as ourselves. We will be the church that says, "No one takes my life but I freely give it," and it's all for LOVE SAKE! And to get here, we must shift from death to life, alive in Christ and dead to sin, worldly desires, and our flesh.

It's when there is a complete understanding of the depth of this never-ending love that your life takes on new meaning. We owe the Father everything, and we should center our lives on giving Him a great return on His investment made in us. Everything Christ did for us had everything to do with this unconditional love we must showcase in the earth, that we may change its trajectory and make a massive impact.

About the Author

Once told, "Your relatability is your superpower!" Prophetess Chrissy Carter has spent the last 20 years transforming hard life lessons into powerful tools to teach, lift, grow and inspire all those she encounters.

She strives daily to be a "Love Agent" of God's Word. Studying HIS word fervently, she uses life experiences to make the Word relatable to all those who hear. Prophetess Carter has learned that sometimes life leads us into unchartered territory, but it's not until we come into the knowledge of Jesus Christ that we have access to the "Road Map." That "Road Map" (the Bible) provides us with enlightenment, healing, and deliverance, ultimately leading us into a Love Dynasty. We are then governed by the precepts of God's unconditional love and reap those benefits.

Prophetess Carter is the wife of Overseer Henry Carter, her life partner and co-laborer of the Gospel. They have a beautiful, blended family consisting of eight children and three grandchildren. Prophetess Carter loves her family and desires them all to be saved, delivered, and living for Jesus. She embraces and is honored to walk out the call God has on her life. Prophetess Carter believes her life's purpose is one of love on assignment-where she uses prayer, intercession, and fasting as the catalyst for the passion behind every message she teaches. Prophetess Carter understands the true power of unconditional love flows through intercession because that same love snatched her out of the darkness. Knowing God can do anything but fail, she strives daily to pour out everything God gives in hopes of winning souls to Christ.

Made in the USA
Columbia, SC
17 February 2022